Dance,
God's *Gift* to You!

Exploring the Origin and Purpose of Dance

Caretha Franks Crawford

Foreword by
Kathy Hazzard

Dance, God's Gift to You!
Exploring the Origin and Purpose of Dance
by Caretha Franks Crawford

Printed in the United States of America

ISBN 9781612154930

Please note that the name satan and related names are not
capitalized. I intentionally did so as not to acknowledge him,
even to the point of violating grammatical rules.

Editorial services by Caletha Crawford, author's daughter

www.xulonpress.com

Dedication

This book is dedicated to the Master of the dance, the Almighty God.

Thank you, Lord, for seeing worth and value in me. You have anointed me to be one of your chosen vessels (a "dust-ball" of the earth) to minister in the dance, and to communicate your heart concerning the dance to others. I am eternally grateful to You for being a loving Father who gives good gifts to His children.

Your dancing daughter,
Caretha

Table of Contents

❧

Acknowledgments

D oing great work for the kingdom of God is never accomplished successfully in isolation. God always provides help, inspiration and encouragement through others.

To those who held up my arms on this journey . . .

Minister Hewlette Pearson, "Thank you" does not adequately express the gratitude I hold in my heart for your inspiration, encouragement and the labor of love you gave to this vision. God will certainly reward you for sharing your intelligence and abilities, which helped to make this book a reality.

In Pursuit of His Presence Worship Institute faculty— Sister Ruth Franks, Elder Pamela Sorrells, First Lady Jeanie Smiling, and Minister Hewlette Pearson—your love for God, His Word, His people and worship are a source of encouragement to me. You give of yourselves assiduously. Thank you for your dedication to the world's greatest worship institute, also known as IPHP.

In Pursuit of His Presence Worship Institute students, your love and hunger for God are the kindling that fuels my fire as I seek to please God and fulfill His awesome mandate "to lay a foundation in the worship arts." You will never know how you are impacting my life and causing me to search diligently for God's richest treasures.

Revealed Dance Ministry and Academy, thank you for providing a place to give birth to the gift of dance God placed in me.

My husband, Pastor Clarence, and daughter, Caletha, thank you for your loving support.

Pastor Chester A. McDonald, Sr., thank you for being a dedicated spiritual father. Your guidance helped to make this vision possible.

Foreword

Finally...a book that tells the REAL story of what dance is all about. Not only does Dr. Caretha Crawford explain the origin of dance, she also gives the reason why the expression is necessary. In one chapter of the book she states, "God sees dancing as a part of and as evidence of restoration." How profound is that statement, especially given the time and season we are in? We are living in a time where some of us are losing things and others are having things taken away, but there is good news! God is restoring to us what the devil can no longer have or control—dance!

Having been in the entertainment business as a singer, actress and model for over 30 years, this book opens up a whole new avenue of understanding regarding "creative expression" in the arts, especially in the realm of what God expects from us as His ultimate creation. I remember the first commercial I ever did...there were people from the "church world" that told me I was going to hell! At that time it was unpopular to wear make-up, go to the movies, wear pants, listen to music (unless it was Christian), and dancing was completely out of the question. Unless you "shouted" (spirited gyration of the body and quick movement of the feet to up-tempo music) in church, anything else your feet did was "sinful!"

I thank God for the insight and revelation, and the courage and fortitude He has given Dr. Caretha Crawford to write this book. She has carefully mapped out, from the beginning to the advent of Christ, what God is expecting in the dance and from those of us in the creative arts ministry and industry. Now that this information is in writing and is here for the "whole" world to see, what will we do now?

There are so many talented and anointed dancers that need to know how the Lord is and will be using them to spread the GOOD NEWS in days and years to come. Jesus Christ has commissioned us to, "Go into all the world and preach the gospel to every creature of the whole human race." That's to every one and everywhere...where the glory of God is needed. Don't get me to start preaching up in here... and when I say, "preach"...I mean to express and communicate...and it includes the dance! This directive is not just for a chosen few...it is to everyone...but look...some of us have not "moved" yet!

I believe there is a clarion call to all marketplace creative ministers. The time is NOW! Daniel and the Hebrew boys showed their skills and were found to be 10 times smarter than their peers. David was skillful in all he did (including soothing a king in torment by playing his harp). And do not forget that David was the one who took off his kingly apparel and danced so hard that some mocked that he was too undignified. Talk about TRUE worship!

There is a verse in the Bible that says, *"A man's gift makes room for him, and brings him before great men."* The gift is what you have to offer...what you come bearing in your hands. From Samson to Solomon, Deborah to Esther... they all came bearing gifts—special skills and talent—to affect their generation; and they did so in a monumental way as their gifts made room for them. Perhaps your obedience to Christ's commission, "Go ye into all the world..." will be through the dance. Can you imagine the doors that will open up to you and the lives you will impact? Wow!

Yes, this book is specifically targeted to the dance, but it will benefit those of us who are in the creative arts. I am the better for the information I have received so far...and now I go forth and..."preach."

So as you read *Dance, God's Gift to You* that Dr. Caretha Crawford has so beautifully written, my hope and prayer are that you will realize and know that God has given each of us an area...talent...skill and more in which to express His glory and splendor.

Could God be waiting on you and asking..."May I have this dance?"

What are you waiting for? Get up and move! Yes, you... move!

Kathy Hazzard
khkathazz@gmail.com

Introduction

This book is a study of the origin and purpose of dance as revealed from the heart of God, the Father. It is not designed to be a historical study of dance in the church. It is a presentation on dance as a gift from God and how we should honor this precious gift. It also serves as a tool to dispel the controversy of whether God is involved in dance.

Controversy is understandable when there is lack of knowledge, and two or more minds have varying views on the subject matter. Knowledge is tantamount to understanding what God has given and ordained to take place in the earth by His people. The Bible states in Hosea 4:6 that God's people are destroyed for lack of knowledge. The word *destroyed* in this verse is the Hebrew word *damah*, and its primitive root means *to be dumb or silent; hence to fail or perish and to be cut off.*[1] Many of God's people, including leaders in the body of Christ, have caused dance, as praise and worship, to be restricted in the Kingdom of God due to lack of knowledge. God has an awesome purpose for dance in His Kingdom, but the uninformed has frustrated His original purpose for dance. When we do not allow God to move or manifest Himself in all areas of praise and worship, we silence or limit that part of God in our individual lives and ministries. As a result, some of what God would like to impart to us is hindered. Many who deny God the opportunity to express Himself through the ministry of dance have forfeited the answer to some of their prayers. As you will come to understand while reading this book, God uses the ministry of dance to change lives and situations. However, God cannot and will not intervene where He is not welcomed in the manner in which He desires to manifest Himself.

This book will present fresh knowledge and revelation concerning the dance. It is written for anyone who desires to hear the Father's heart on the subject of dance. However, pastors, ministry leaders and ministers of the dance are particularly encouraged to read and meditate on the material presented. Before you read, pray and ask the Holy Spirit to open the eyes of your understanding that you might receive the truth that has been revealed in this book. Lay aside all that you think you know about dance, and approach it with an open mind as you allow the Holy Spirit to teach you truth that can revolutionize your life, and the lives of the people in your circle of influence. John 8:32 states, *"And ye shall know the truth, and the truth shall make you free."* Truth is liberating power! Truth opens our minds so that we can receive and apply new knowledge.

The objective of this book is to unveil the origin of dance, the purpose for which it was created; and to define how dance is to be used today to reveal God's glory in the earth. In addition, considerable time will be spent on what God expects of those involved in the ministry of the dance. *Dance, God's Gift to You* explores topics such as: Me, Called to Dance?; There is Power in the Feet; Characteristics of the Dance Minister; Are You a Worshipper?; The Importance of the Anointing; A Word for the Fifty-Something Plus; Your Appearance Matters; Dancers as Servants; and The Power of Unity.

Chapter One

Me, Called to Dance?

"Life may not be the party we hoped for, but while we're here we should dance."
—Anonymous

People of all nationalities and ethnicities seem to enjoy dancing. There are different types and styles of dancing: folk, social, ballroom, disco, hip hop, ballet, tap, jig, salsa, break dancing, waltz, tango, step and liturgical, just to name a few. As you will come to understand, dancing has been around for ages. However, it seems that dance has become quite popular and a part of every day life in the 21st century. Its popularity has grown possibly due to the advancement of technology that literally puts the world at our fingertips. Because of the media, we are able to watch "stars" feature their talent on a weekly basis on *Dancing with the Stars*, a popular television program in the United States. Dancing seems to bring such joy and satisfaction to the soul. Dance, for most people—especially people of color—is as natural as breathing. It seems to be an innate response to music.

From a child, I have always loved to dance, but dancing was taboo in our home when I was growing up.

My mother, who embraced the holiness religion, believed that any dancing—other than what the church referred to as "shouting"—was of the devil, or carnal and worldly. However, her convictions only cramped my style. But whenever I had the opportunity, and she was not looking, I danced.

One of my most hurtful childhood memories involved dance. When I was in the fourth grade, all the little girls in the class participated in a homecoming parade dance routine and I was not allowed to join them. As you can possibly imagine, this burned a painful memory in my soul. The prom was no exception as this caused drama, but my father intervened and I was allowed to attend . . . yes, I danced!

Many years later, God revealed to me how He used my mother as a buffer to protect the anointing on my life. In essence my mother's way of curtailing my dance activities prevented me from getting caught up and going deeper into worldly dance. I had no clue (and neither did my mother) that God had a call on my life to minister in the dance. It has taken many years of not knowing what was going on...the "whys"...and the fact that God had a purpose in not allowing some things to occur. I did not have the knowledge that God uses things to vet and stir me in a certain direction in order to keep me from going off a certain path, and to accomplish His plan for my life. Thank God, for His infinite wisdom because there was a purpose in the pain which orchestrated the process of what would later be ministry.

Can you imagine how elated I was when God revealed to me that He had not only anointed me to minister in the dance, but to teach others matters of His heart concerning dance? I was sitting in our church at a pastoral anniversary service in 2003, when the Lord gave me a vision of myself dancing in the pulpit. When I finished dancing, someone threw me the microphone and I started preaching again. Whoa! Talk about an "Aha" moment! A few minutes later, after the vision, the Holy Spirit literally took my arms and started moving them in dance motions. It felt so graceful and beautiful. I hadn't realized that other's had noticed, but after the service, several people mentioned to me that they saw me doing liturgical dancing. I thought about the possibility of a call to the dance ministry, but after musing over the thought for a few hours, I stored it in the back of my mind.

It was not until three years later that I embraced the call. Again, I was sitting in a service and just before I was to preach, the pastor's daughter ministered in the dance. As she began to minister, it was as if her spirit witnessed to my spirit that I was called to the ministry of the dance. It was a Mary and Elizabeth moment. The "baby" leaped on the inside of me. I instantly made up my mind that I had to deliver the "baby" of dance. During my closing remarks at the service, I made a bold declaration and announced my calling. I did not want to give the enemy a chance to mess with my mind with doubt and fear, so I immediately approached the dance minister about the possibility of enrolling in their academy.

Though the academy was closed, I did not allow this to prevent me from moving forward. I patiently waited on God for the next step. Let me pause here and encourage you with a thought . . . God is preparing the perfect place for the birth of your "baby." Mary, the mother of Jesus, had a designated place in Bethlehem. This place was prophesied thousands of years before Jesus was born. Your "Bethlehem" is being prepared. Wait on it. Many talk about waiting on "your Boaz," but I encourage you to also wait on your birthing place. In time God will reveal and make the right connections.

About a year later, I had the privilege of attending a ministers' fellowship where I met the founder and director of a dance academy. I thought to myself, "This cannot be happenstance." I shared with the group that God had called me to the dance ministry and I was waiting on God for further direction. The dance director laid her hand on my thigh and said, "Don't let that dance die in you." I knew this was a word from God. She later invited me to her upcoming seminar and night of dance. I attended and ministered at the night of dance. This connection later grew into my serving as a dance minister, instructor and chaplain for the ministry.

To God be the glory! He provided my "Bethlehem."

Chapter Two

Dance: What Is It?

"Dancing is like dreaming with your feet!"
—Constanze

D ance, as defined by *Webster's New World Dictionary, Third College Edition*, means to move the body and feet in rhythm, ordinarily to music, to move lightly and gaily; caper, to bob up and down, to be stirred into rapid movement, as leaves in a wind.[1] The *Encyclopedia Britannica Online* defines dance as a form of expression that uses bodily movement that are rhythmic, patterned (or sometimes improvised), and usually accompanied by music.[2]

The English word "dance" and its forms (dancing, danced and dances) are found 27 times in the King James version of the Bible. Since the original writings of the Bible were primarily written in Hebrew and Greek, an overview of the word translated as "dance" and all of its forms will be presented in these languages.

Hebrew Words:
- **Chuwl**, *khool*,or **chiyl**, *kheel*, (Strong's 2342) to twist or whirl (in a circular or spiral manner), i.e.

specifically to dance, to writhe in pain, to bring forth, to travail. (Judges 21:21,23)

- **Karar**, *kaw-rar*, (Strong's 3769) to dance (i.e. whirl): dance, dancing. (2 Samuel 6:14, 16)
- **Machowl**, *maw-khole*, (Strong's 4234, from 2342) a (round) dance:–dance (-cing). (Psalm 143:3; 150:4; Jeremiah 31:13; Lamentations 5:15; Psalm 30:11).
- **Machowlah**, *mekh-o-law*; (Strong's 4246, feminine of 4234); a dance:–company, dances (cing). (Exodus 15:20, 32:19; Judges 11:34; 1 Samuel 21:11; 3 other occurrences)
- **Raqad**, *raw-kad*, (Strong's 7540) a primitive root; prop, to stomp, i.e. to spring about (wildly or for joy):–dance, jump, leap, skip). (Job 21:11; Ecclesiastes 3:4; Isaiah 13:21; 1 Chronicles 15:29)
- **Chagag**, *khaw-gag*, (Strong's 2287) to move in a circle, i.e., specifically to march in a sacred procession, to observe a festival; by implication, to be giddy:–celebrate, dance, (keep, hold) a (solemn) feast (holiday), reel to and fro. (1 Samuel 30:16)

Greek Words:
- **Orxeomai**, orcheomai, or *or-kheh-om-ahee*, (Strong's 3738) from *orchos* (a row or ring); to dance (from the ranklike or regular motion);–dance. (Matthew 11:17, 14:6; Mark 6:22; Luke 7:32)
- **Xoros**, choros, *khor-os*, (Strong's 5525) a ring, i.e. round dance ("choir"): –dancing. (Luke 15:25)

As you can see from the Hebrew and Greek terms, dancing involves movement, whether it is jumping, skipping, leaping, stomping, marching, bobbing or reeling back and forth. Dancing can be done in different formations: circular, in a row or line, processional or by rank.

The following are other words, which convey dancing and movement:

- *Frolic*
- *Jump*
- *Skip*
- *Bounce*
- *Prance*
- *Stomp*
- *Sway*
- *Whirl*
- *Twist*
- *Spin*
- *Swing*
- *Caper*
- *Jig*
- *Leap*
- *Clap*
- *Shout*
- *To celebrate*
- *To rejoice*
- *To stroll*
- *To extend the hands*
- *To jump for joy*
- *To perform*
- *To boast.*

Other Hebrew Words that Convey Dancing:

- **Yadah,** *yaw-daw,* (Strong's 3034) to revere or worship with extended hands, to throw, an expression of thanks. Over one hundred occurrences in the Old Testament. (Psalm 7:17, 9:1, 108:3)
- **Halal,** *haw-lal,* (Strong's 1984) to make a show, to boast; and thus to be (clamorously) foolish; to rave, to celebrate. (1 Chronicles 23:30; Psalm 149:3; 150:1)

- **Towdah**, *to-daw,* (Strong's 8426) an extension of the hands expressing adoration; specifically, a choir of worshippers, a sacrifice of praise, thanksgiving. (Jeremiah 17:26, 33:11; Psalm 50:23)
- **Giyl,** *gheel,* or **guwl**, *gool,* (Strong's 1523) to spin round (under the influence of any violent emotion), i.e. usually rejoice, or (as cringing) fear:–be glad, joy, be joyful, rejoice. It gives the idea of dancing for joy or leaping for joy. (Psalm 2:11, 51:8, 53:6; Psalm 35:9; Isaiah 49:13; Psalm 31:7, 96:11)
- **Alaz**, *aw-laz,* (Strong's 5937) to jump for joy, i.e. exult:–be joyful, rejoice, triumph. (Psalm 60:6, 68:4, 96:12, 149:5; Isaiah 23:12; Habakkuk 3:18)

Other Greek Words that Convey Dancing:
- **Agalliao**, *ag-al-lee-ah-o,* (Strong's 21) to jump for joy, i.e. exult:–be (exceeding) glad, with exceeding joy, rejoice (greatly). (Luke 1:47, 10:21; John 5:35, 8:56; Acts 16:34; 1 Peter 1:6, 8; Revelation 19:7)
- **Skirtao**, *skeer-tah-o,* (Strong's 4640) to skip; to jump, i.e. sympathetically move (as the quickening of a fetus):–leap (for joy). (Luke 1:41, 1:44; 6:23)
- **Hallomai**, *hal-lom-ahee,* (Strong's 242) to jump; figuratively, to gush:–leap, spring up. (John 4:14; Acts 3:8, 14:10)

This is not an exhaustive list of Hebrew and Greek words; however, as you consider the meaning of each word and examine the references, it can be clearly seen that dance is a verb. It requires action . . . it is movement. Also note that joy and rejoicing are associated with the term dance.

Dance is Joyful

In Ecclesiastes 3:4, Solomon does the antithesis of dancing: mourning.

A time to weep, and a time to laugh; a time to mourn, and a time to dance.

Since mourning denotes sadness and grief, dancing, therefore, indicates gladness and joy. Furthermore, God promises believers in Isaiah 61:3 that if we would give Him our mourning, that is, our grief and sadness, He would divinely exchange it for the oil of joy.

To appoint unto them that mourn in Zion, to give unto them beauty for ashes, the oil of joy for mourning, the garment of praise for the spirit of heaviness; that they might be called trees of righteousness, the planting of the LORD, that he might be glorified.

God is literally saying that He will replace the sadness and grief of mourning by anointing us with joy and gladness. *Anointing* means to smear or to rub; it empowers. When God anoints us with the oil of joy, we will not just merely have joy, but we will walk in the power of joy and rejoicing; and they will control our very being. Therefore, grief and sadness will lose the grip that they once held.

The book of Esther illustrates this point of mourning and rejoicing. Haman, the king's second in command, plotted against the Jews, God's chosen people, to have them annihilated. A decree went out from the king to this effect. Mordecai, Esther's uncle, learned about the plot and went into mourning clothed in sackcloth and ashes. As the news reached the various provinces, they mourned as well.

When Mordecai perceived all that was done,
Mordecai rent his clothes, and put on sackcloth with
ashes, and went out into the midst of the city, and
cried with a loud and a bitter cry; And came even
before the king's gate: for none might enter into the
king's gate clothed with sackcloth. And in every province, whithersoever the king's commandment and
his decree came, there was great mourning among
the Jews, and fasting, and weeping, and wailing; and
many lay in sackcloth and ashes.
—Esther 4:13

However, Esther took a risk in going to see the king, as
it was unlawful for the queen to come into the royal court
without being summoned by him. She entered on behalf
of her people and the king granted her favor. He learned
the truth about why Haman wanted the Jews annihilated.
Haman's plot turned on him and he was caught in his own
trap. The king sent out another decree that gave the Jews permission to protect themselves from their enemies. The whole
city and the Jews rejoiced.

And Mordecai went out from the presence of the
king in royal apparel of blue and white, and with
a great crown of gold, and with a garment of fine
linen and purple: and the city of Shushan *rejoiced*
and was glad. The Jews had light, and gladness, and
joy, and honour. And in every province, and in every
city, whithersoever the king's commandment and his
decree came, the Jews had *joy* and gladness, a feast
and a good day. And many of the people of the land
became Jews; for the fear of the Jews fell upon them.
—Esther 8:15-17, emphasis added

Here again we see the antithesis of mourning and rejoicing. God turned their mourning to joy and gladness; and they celebrated with a feast of which dancing was an integral part.

God further states in Isaiah 61:3 that He would lift our heavy spirit and place on us a garment of praise. A heavy spirit is a bowed-down, defeated spirit of hopelessness. But God said He would strip us of that spirit and place on us a garment that praises. Instead of walking around in despair, we will go about rejoicing and praising.

David further encourages us as he expresses gratitude to God for turning his mourning into dancing:

Thou hast turned for me my mourning into dancing: thou hast put off my sackcloth, and girded me with gladness.

—Psalm 30:11

In this section of his dedicatory prayer, we can see how David contrasted mourning and dancing. He further elaborates by stating that God had taken off his sackcloth (a symbol of grief and mourning) and clothed him with gladness.

Most of us have mourned, perhaps, the death of a loved one or when we have been emotionally and physically wounded. At those times our spirit was broken and we became physically weak. In some cases we were so sad and despondent, we did not think we could move forward in life. But there is something beautiful about the verse we just read. At first glance, this verse seems to offer—what seem to be difficult to do in those sad times—an answer to mourning. However, a closer look reveals that God is the one who does the "turning," the "putting off," and the "putting on." When we are faced with those difficult times, He knows what joy and gladness does to the spirit. He also knows that the physical act of movement—dance—is directly associated with the spirit of joy and gladness. So He turns our crying into dancing, assists us in taking off the heavy spirit that has us bowed down, and gives us clothes that resonate with gladness, laughter and joy!

What is wonderful about this is that our low times do not need to last long. David also states in the Psalm, *". . . Weeping may endure for a night, but joy cometh in the morning."* Clearly we can see from these Scriptures that grief and mourning is the opposite of joy and gladness. We can therefore conclude that dance is joyful.

Previously, I stated that "to rejoice" is a term that can convey dancing; it is a synonym for dance. One of the Hebrew words translated numerous times as *"to rejoice"* is *Samach* according to *Vine's Expository Dictionary of Biblical Words.*

> *Samach* usually refers to a spontaneous emotion or extreme happiness, which is expressed in some visible and or external manner. It does not normally represent an abiding state of well-being or feeling. This emotion arises at festivals, circumcision feasts, wedding feasts, harvest feasts, the overthrow of one's enemies, and other such events. The men of Jabesh broke out *joyously* when they were told that they would be delivered from the Philistines. 1 Sam 11:9

> The emotion expressed in the verb samach usually finds a visible expression. In Jer 50:11 the Babylonians are denounced as being glad and "jubilant" over the pillage of Israel. Their emotion is expressed externally by their skipping about like a threshing heifer and neighing like stallions. The emotion represented in the verb (and concretized in the noun simchah) is sometimes accompanied by dancing, singing and playing musical instruments. This was the sense when David was heralded by the

women of Jerusalem as he returned victorious over the Philistines 1 Sam 18:6. This emotion is usually described as the product of some external situation, circumstance, or experience, such as found in the first biblical appearance of samach: God told Moses that Aaron was coming to meet him and "when he seeth thee, he will be *glad in his heart*" Ex 4:14. This passage speaks of inner feeling which is visibly expressed. When Aaron saw Moses, he was *overcome with joy* and kissed him v. 27.

Therefore, the verb samach suggests three elements: (1) a spontaneous, unsustained *feeling of jubilance*, (2) a feeling so strong that it finds expression in some external act, and (3) a feeling prompted by some external and unsustained stimulus.[3]

> —Emphasis added

Numerous times in the Scriptures, God commands us to "rejoice." He wants us to be joyful—leaping, whirling, skipping, clapping, singing and dancing—showing our emotions in a way that glorifies Him. However, in many church circles, it is taught or implied that we are to be stoic. We should bury or constrain the emotions God gave us for our own well-being and for His delight.

In the Old Testament, God commanded His people, Israel, to have festivals, which incorporated (consist of) showing their emotions.

And ye shall take you on the first day the boughs of goodly trees, branches of palm trees, and the boughs of thick trees, and willows of the brook; and ye shall *rejoice* before the LORD your God seven days.

> —Leviticus 23:40, emphasis added

Seven days shalt thou keep a solemn feast unto the
LORD thy God in the place which the LORD shall
choose: because the LORD thy God shall bless thee
in all thine increase, and in all the works of thine
hands, therefore thou shalt surely *rejoice.*
>   —Deut 16:15, emphasis added

And thou shalt *rejoice* in every good thing which the
LORD thy God hath given unto thee, and unto thine
house, thou, and the Levite, and the stranger that is
among you.
>   —Deut 26:11, emphasis added

God appointed special days for His people to bask in and
show appreciation for Him and what He had done for them.
It makes God's heart glad when we are happy, healthy and
whole the way He always intended us to be. Remember, we
are made in the image of God, and we possess His character
. . . His nature. A part of His nature is joy and delight, and if
we are truly walking in the image of God, we have to be a
delightful people, full of joy and vigor.

Habakkuk made a decision to be joyful. At the end of
the day, after he poured out his complaint to God about the
wickedness around him, he made a decision that it did not
matter about the circumstances around him, he was going to
not only have joy, but also express it.

Although the fig tree shall not blossom, neither shall
fruit be in the vines; the labour of the olive shall fail,
and the fields shall yield no meat; the flock shall be
cut off from the fold, and there shall be no herd in the
stalls: Yet I will *rejoice* in the LORD, I will *joy* in the
God of my salvation.
>   —Hebrew 3:17-18, emphasis added

The Hebrew word for *joy* is *gil*—suggests spinning, leaping, whirling and dancing with intense emotion. It was not until after Habakkuk had an encounter with the living God that he decided he would be joyful and express gratitude to the God of his salvation. The introduction to his prayer in chapter three, "A prayer of Habakkuk the prophet, on Shigionoth," suggests that it was set to wild and enthusiastic music accompanied by great excitement. According to some sources, the exact meaning of "Shigionoth" is unknown, but it does indicate a type of music notation.

When we encounter God, we will do like Habakkuk and rejoice in Him with uninhibited emotions. We bring delight to God's heart when we humble ourselves and glorify Him through our emotions. King David is another example of a man who threw caution to the wind, so to speak, and danced wildly and enthusiastically before the Lord when the Ark of the Covenant was being brought back to Jerusalem. He did not allow pride or criticism by his wife to abort his joy and rejoicing in the Lord.

There are many Scriptures in the New Testament that command us to "rejoice."

Rejoice in the Lord alway: and again I say, Rejoice.
— Philippians 4:4

Rejoice evermore.
— 1 Thessalonians 5:16

But rejoice, inasmuch as ye are partakers of Christ's sufferings; that, when his glory shall be revealed, ye may be glad also with exceeding joy.
— 1 Peter 4:13

Finally, my brethren, rejoice in the Lord.
— Philippians 3:1

The reason for rejoicing was made very clear in Nehemiah 8:10:

> Then he said unto them, Go your way, eat the fat, and drink the sweet, and send portions unto them for whom nothing is prepared: for this day is holy unto our Lord: neither be ye sorry; *for the joy of the LORD is your strength.*
>
> —Emphasis added

Rejoicing is also the mood in heaven. The heavenly host rejoiced at Christ's birth. The long awaited moment had finally arrived; peace and good will had come to earth.

> And suddenly there was with the angel a multitude of the heavenly host praising God, and saying, Glory to God in the highest, and on earth peace, good will toward men.
>
> —Luke 2:13-14

Dance, what is it? We have just learned that it is joyful, celebratory; involves ecstatic motion and is used to lift the spirit and bring strength. I defined dance from its English, Hebrew and Greek perspective and shared the impact that it has on one's emotional, physical and spiritual well being. However, I will elaborate further on the importance of dance from God's perspective. Before praise and worship dance can be distinguished, we need to know who created dance and for what purpose.

Think On These Things

After reading *Dance: What Is It?*, I have a better
understanding of . . .

_____

_____

_____

_____

_____

_____

_____

_____

_____

_____

_____

_____

_____

_____

_____

_____

_____

_____

_____

_____

_____

_____

_____

_____

_____

_____

_____

Chapter Three

The Creator of the Dance
and Its Purpose

"I would believe only in a God that knows how to dance."
—Friedrich Nietzsche

When theologians grapple with the question of the existence of God, they usually begin from the argument of general revelation—the universal ways in which God reveals Himself to mankind. There are commonly five means or arguments of general revelation. One is known as the *teleological argument*, which is the study of final causes, end or evidences. This argument states that the order and design that we observe in our world has an ultimate purpose and necessitates a designer. Not just any designer, however, but a Mastermind. Many use the illustration of a watch to present this evidence. It is argued that a watch must not only have a maker, but also a designer. Any one can make a watch once an initial pattern or design is made, however, there had to be a master designer who invented or created the pattern for the watch; and with its purpose in mind. In other words, the designer had a definite function for the watch.

The watch did not haphazardly appear on the earth. Think about it, when we look at a watch we see what it does, but we do not realize the complexities of the parts that move in conjunction with each other to provide the accuracy of time. As a result, its purpose required its creation.

Likewise, dance did not appear on the earth by chance. Its purpose necessitated its creation. When one views the dance, we can appreciate the movement and the immediate impact it has on our emotions, however, as with the watch, there are inner workings that are taking place that are not visible to the naked eye. These inner workings include, but are not limited to, spiritual warfare, healing, deliverance and restoration. There is a reverberation that takes place as earth summons heaven and heaven responds with a climatic answer.

As you very well know, whenever God does or creates something, it is for a distinct purpose. The Bible, the only divinely inspired Word of God, reveals this. He is the originator and creator of all things. As John declares,

All things were made by Him [God]; and without Him was not any thing made that was made.
—John 1:3

The Amplified Version states,

All things were made *and* came into existence through Him . . .

The "Him" that is referred to is God, Jesus Christ.

There are other Scriptures that confirm that God is the creator of all things:

For by Him were all things created, that are in heaven, and that are in earth, visible and invisible, whether

they be thrones, or dominions, or principalities, or
powers: all things were created by Him, and for Him.
—Colossians 1:16

For from Him and through Him and to Him are all
things. [For all things originate with Him and come
from Him; all things live through Him, and all things
center in and tend to consummate and to end in Him.]
To Him be glory forever! Amen (so be it).
—Romans 11:36 (AMP)

What a great way to end the passage in Romans refer-
enced above. God has settled it Himself that He is the originator of all things, which includes the dance. God said it, and
whether we believe it or not the case is closed.

Just as the watch required an intelligent mind to design
it for its purpose, likewise, dance has been divinely created
to fulfill a purpose. The watch is necessary to capture how
time moves along, so worship in comparison, allows us to
capture the heart of God and what He is saying and doing in
the earth today. Worship through dance is as much a part of
the worship experience that we give unto the Father. Now
that we know what dance is and who created it, now let us
look at its purpose.

Purpose answers the "why" question. Many of us know
Dr. Myles Munroe of the Bahamas as the "purpose" teacher,
as you might have heard his teachings on purpose or read his
books. He has a saying that if you don't know the purpose of
a thing, you will ultimately abuse it—that is, misuse it. Dr.
Munroe shares that, "Until purpose is discovered, existence
has no meaning, for purpose is the source of fulfillment."[1]

Dance, in many instances, is being abused because of
misunderstanding of its purpose. Although dance is beautiful
artistry, it is much more than that. Many are dancing, however, is God's purpose being fulfilled?

Revelation 4:11 sheds some light on the "why" question.

Thou art worthy, O Lord, to receive glory and honour and power: for thou hast created all things, and for thy pleasure they are and were created.

God created all things for HIS PLEASURE. The term pleasure in this passage is the Greek term, *thelema*. It means determination, choice, purpose, decree, inclination, desire, pleasure and will. God created dance by His own will. Some synonyms for pleasure are: enjoyment, delight, joy, gratification, happiness and contentment. Think about it . . . God created dance for His own enjoyment and delight. He is happy and content with dance when it brings glory to His name. (See Psalm 149:3-4.) Dance gratifies Him and gives Him satisfaction. It is one of God's precious jewels. Because we know that God created dance for His own delight and enjoyment, let us see how and why it brings Him great satisfaction

A Mighty Tool In His Hands

God used dance as a mighty instrument in creation and restoration. He used dance to bring order to a chaotic earth. Let us go back to the beginning of the Bible and examine Genesis 1:1-2.

In the beginning God created the heaven and the earth. And the earth was without form and void; and darkness was upon the face of the deep. And the Spirit of God moved upon the face of the waters.

The word *created* in this passage is the Hebrew term *bara* (baw-raw). It means to bring in to existence, to produce, make, put in form, renew, to cut down.[2] God, the all-powerful One, is the only subject of this verb; because He is the only

One who can produce something out of nothing. The word *bara* was used in antiquity to mean *cut down*, expressing or giving the idea of *carving* or *fashioning*. Therefore Genesis 1:1 is stating that God fashioned or produced the heavens and the earth without any previously existing material or matter.

However, according to Genesis 1:2, when God looked at the earth, it was without form and void. *"Form"* in this passage is the Hebrew term *tohuw, (to'hoo)*. It means to lie waste; desert, empty place, barren, confusion, vain; therefore, lacking order or arrangement.[3] *Void* in this passage is the Hebrew term *"bohuw, bohoo"* which means to be empty; an undistinguishable ruin.[4] Genesis 1:2 also states that "darkness was upon the deep." *Deep* is the Hebrew term *"teh-home"* which means an abyss—as a surging mass of water.[5] The waters were dark, void of light. The earth that God had fashioned laid waste, empty, dark, without order; it existed in a state of chaos.

I imagine many theologians and scholars would disagree with this statement. Many teach and believe that there was a major cataclysmic event caused by Lucifer's fall that took place between Genesis 1:1 and Genesis 1:2, that threw the earth into a chaotic state. This theory is known as the "gap theory." How the chaotic state came into being is irrelevant to this study. The point is the earth was in a chaotic state, whether as a result of the original creative process or of Lucifer's interference. And God used dance as an instrument to bring and/or restore order in the earth. Dance was God's aid in creation, and He brought order out of chaos through the dance.

God was not delighted with an earth that lacked order and beauty, as it did not bring Him pleasure. According to Genesis 1:2, *"the Spirit of God moved upon the face of the waters."* The Spirit of God is the Holy Spirit, and "moved" means that He danced or hovered over the waters.

Remember, dance is movement. The Holy Spirit is a person and He moved or danced upon the face of the waters while God commanded light to come forth— *"Let there be light"* (Genesis 1:3)—and darkness vanished. That which was once chaotic came into alignment; order was established according to the perfect will of God. His will was to have an earth with form filled with His light and beauty. Thus the earth was created—order came into existence—with God speaking and dancing.

There were other activities taking place while God was laying the foundations of the earth. According to Job 38:7, the stars and angels were celebrating. When God answered Job out of the whirlwind, God wanted to know from Job,

> Where were you when I laid the foundations of the earth?
> —Job 38:4a

He continued His interrogation,

> When the morning stars sang together, and all the sons of God shouted for joy?
> —Job 38:7

The stars were singing and the sons of God, that is the angels, were shouting when God laid the foundations of the earth. Remember, shouting is a synonym for dancing. Whether shouting with their voices or making movements with their bodies, a joyous celebration was occurring. Dancing, speaking, singing and shouting were taking place as the foundations of the earth were being laid. This sounds like a glorious event to me, and one that only God could have orchestrated.

The "First Mentioned" Sets the Pattern

There is a law called "The Law of First-Mention." This law simply means that whenever something or a subject matter is first mentioned in the Bible, the concept, principle or idea that it conveys remains throughout the Bible. For example, the first mention of marriage in the Bible is between a man and a woman. This sets the pattern for marriage. Throughout the Bible holy matrimony is between a man and a woman, there is no deviation. When other patterns are presented as marriage, they are rejected and abhorred by our Holy Father who instituted marriage.

The first mention of dance in the Bible is in Genesis 1:2 when the Holy Spirit danced over the waters (this is the seed from which all dance springs). In this instance, God is dancing as an agent in creating or recreating. The point being that throughout the Bible, whenever dance is mentioned, except when it is perverted or corrupted, it is for God's creative purpose.

From Genesis 1:2 forward, each time dance occurs, God is creating, re-creating, renewing, refashioning, refreshing, reviving, reestablishing, reconditioning, reconstructing, reinstating or reinstalling something. Order was established, order came out of chaos. The earth was in a state of confusion and God used dance to bring it back into alignment. As you can see dance, pure dance brought the earth into alignment to the will of God.

Think On These Things

After reading *The Creator of the Dance and Its Purpose*,
I now understand . . .

_____

_____

_____

_____

_____

_____

_____

_____

_____

_____

_____

_____

_____

_____

_____

_____

_____

_____

_____

_____

_____

_____

_____

_____

_____

Chapter Four

Biblical God-Inspired Dancing

"There are two ways of being creative. One can sing and dance. Or one can create an environment in which singers and dancers flourish."
— Warren G. Bennis

There are many instances in the Bible where God used dance for His purposes. In Exodus 15:20 we find the English word dance for the first time in the Bible.

> And Miriam the prophetess, the sister of Aaron, took a timbrel in her hand; and all the women went out after her with timbrels and with dances.

This celebration took place after the children of Israel crossed the Red Sea. Moses led the congregation in a praise song unto the Lord, and Miriam and all the women used timbrels to make music and they danced. This dance was prophetic, spontaneous and prompted by the Holy Spirit. God stirred the message of triumph, victory and joy in Miriam's heart and she expressed it through the dance. While Moses' expression was that of song.

They also danced a dance of victory. The children of Israel had accomplished their goal; they had been delivered from slavery and gained great victory over the enemy. It was a triumphant dance where God demonstrated His power and authority over the Egyptians. Furthermore, it was a dance of salvation and deliverance. Israel had been redeemed from destruction and freed from the bondage of slavery. Ultimately, it was a dance of praise. The people of God were rejoicing and thanking God for what He had done for them.

How was God pleased by the dance? Because God inhabits the praises of His people; it drew Him in their midst as Moses and Miriam led the people in worship. God had a place where He could sit. Furthermore, in celebrating God's goodness to them, they prophetical fulfilled God's command in Psalm 150.

> Praise ye the LORD . . . Praise Him for His mighty acts: praise Him according to His excellent greatness . . . Praise Him with the timbrel and dance . . . Let everything that hath breath praise the LORD. Praise ye the LORD.
>
> —vv. 1-6

Their obedience brought pleasure to God. Moreover, God was taking pleasure in the fact that order was coming back to His people. The nation of Israel, God's chosen people, was out of place, thus, out of order in Egypt. Egypt was not the ordained place that God had assigned for them. They could never experience the fullness of their blessings under the rulership of another master.

The dance led by Miriam was a visual manifestation of what God was doing with His people—bringing order out of chaos. God was taking His rightful place with His people as their Lord and Master. He was renewing, reviving, refreshing, redeeming and reestablishing them as His people. And God used dance as an instrument of restoration. Egypt was no longer holding them captive and the transformation process was now in place—the nation was coming into proper alignment with their God.

Other Victory Dances

In Israel and the Near East, it was customary to celebrate victory over the enemy with dance. The children of Israel found themselves in battle against the enemy on many occasions. One such occasion is reported in the 11th chapter of Judges—the battle against the Ammonites. Jephthah was chosen as the commander of Israel's army, and God gave him the strategy for victory. Jephthah, wanting to show gratitude to God for an impending victory, made a foolish vow to God. He promised to offer up to God whatever came out of his house to meet him upon his return from a victorious battle with the Ammonites. Surprisingly, his only daughter came out to greet him when he returned home. She celebrated her father's victory with tambourine and dancing.

During the days of the Judges, Israel was in a rebellious cycle. They would sin against God; God would allow their enemies to oppress them; they would cry out to God in repentance; and God would rescue them. This—the children of Israel versus the Ammonites—was another one of those occasions. God had done more than merely deliver His people from the hand of the enemy, as a result of this victory their hearts were returned to the covenant that God had established with them. Dance was used as an outward expression of what God had done.

We see a similar scenario in the 18th chapter of 1 Samuel. King Saul and David returned home from fighting Israel's archenemy, the Philistines. The women came out to greet them in celebration.

And it came to pass as they came, when David was
returned from the slaughter of the Philistine, that the
women came out of all cities of Israel, singing and
dancing, to meet king Saul, with tabrets, with joy,
and with instruments of music.

—1 Samuel 18:6

Again we have a celebration of victory and thanksgiving
led by the women. And once more God reconfirms His
power and position in the lives of His people, Israel. In both
instances—Jephthah and the Ammonites, and King Saul and
the Philistines—the results were realignment. Once more,
dance was used to bring order out of chaos.

Dance: Not for Women Only

One of the most memorable celebrations in the Bible in
which dance was used in restoration was initiated by Israel's
greatest king, King David. In 2 Samuel 6, King David
attempted to bring the Ark of the Lord to Jerusalem. The
Ark of the Lord was the presence of God among His people.
It was used to give direction and guidance to the Israelites.
During the judgeship of the priest Eli, Israel fought against
the Philistines and the Ark was stolen. It remained in the land
of the Philistines for seven months. It was later recaptured
by the Israelites and remained in the house of Abinadab for
20 years. (See 1 Samuel 4, 5, 6 and 7.) During this time, the
Israelites lamented for God; they had a strong desire for His
presence.

When David was made king over all of Israel, he, along
with the leadership of Israel, decided it was time for the
Ark to be in Jerusalem among God's people. King David's
first attempt to retrieve the Ark of God from the house of
Abinadab ended in tragedy and grief because of improper
handling of the Ark. Because of that tragedy, David became

angry and afraid to move the Ark, so it rested in the house of Obed-Edom for three months. After which, King David and the house of Israel went down and retrieved the Ark of God.

David was so excited and filled with joy as the Ark was being transported to Jerusalem that he made sacrifices and danced before the Lord.

> And it was so, that when they that bare the ark of the LORD had gone six paces, he sacrificed oxen and fatlings. And David danced before the LORD with all his might; and David was girded with a linen ephod. So David and all the house of Israel brought up the ark of the LORD with shouting, and with the sound of the trumpet.
> —2 Second Samuel 6:13-15

David's dancing could be described as enthusiastic and wild; some translations of the Bible said that he leaped and whirled. King David put all of his being into praising God through the dance, so much so that he uncovered himself in front of the women—he took off his outer garment (2 Samuel 6:20). A loud celebration of instrument playing and dancing accompanied the return of the Ark to Israel.

Here again we see how God's people used dance for praise, worship, victory, triumph and deliverance. When the priests and the Levites (singers, musicians, dancers, and shouters of joy) were transporting the Ark to it's rightful place, King David danced enthusiastically. God's desire was to dwell among His people and in turn they would be comforted by His presence. However this could not be while the Ark was in the hands of the Philistines, which brought chaos and a state of confusion to God's people. King David's dance was used by God as a means of bringing order, restoration and worship protocol to Israel. God's purpose and will for the Ark had come back into alignment. God reestablished

His presence among His people; thus, bringing pleasure to His heart.

Restoration of a Household

Although the word "order" has been abused in many circles, especially in the church, God's way is still *order*—the pattern or paradigm that He has established to accomplish His will in the earth. God never intended for the earth to be out of alignment.

God established order in all of His creation, even in the galaxies. The planets, sun, moon and stars all exist and operate in divinely established alignment. The seasons also operate in order. All institutions established by God have order: the family is the first of such institutions and Paul elaborates on its divine order in Ephesians 5:22-33, 6:1-4.

We see an example of disorder in a family in the story of the prodigal son found in Luke 15:11-32. The word *prodigal* means squanderer, waster and shortsightedness. The younger son in this parable exhibited all these attributes, as he was a person of little to no wisdom. Because of his shortsightedness, he removed himself from under the guidance and wisdom of his father; went to a far country and wasted his inheritance. He took a dramatic turn for the worse as disorder ruled his life.

After losing all his money and so-called friends, a severe famine hit the land. With needs and no resources, he found himself in a shameful and forbidden place according to Jewish standards. He was hired to feed pigs (which are unclean animals; Jews were forbidden to touch or be in the presence of swine), and no one gave him anything. This was his only means of survival and he would have eaten the pig's food, but he suddenly came to the realization that his father's house had more than enough to spare.

Although the son operated in disorder (by disrespecting and dishonoring the order established in his family) the father never gave up hope on his younger son. He expected his son to come back into proper alignment one day. The father knew what it would take to seal this event. Upon seeing his son in the distance he immediately executed his plan: he ran toward his son and welcomed him heartily. After all the kissing, hugging, confessing, and giving of gifts, the father called for the servants to prepare the long awaited party. They killed and roasted the calf (that was being especially prepared for the occasion), ate, drank and made merriment with music and dancing.

In preparation for his son's return, the father ensured that dancing and music were a part of the restoration celebration. We can see how dancing played a major role in restoring this family unit to proper order. The son was revived, accepted and restored to his former position.

> It was meet [necessary] that we should make merry, and be glad: for this thy brother was dead, and is alive again; and was lost, and is found.
>   —Luke 15:32

This was a celebration of victory; the son had been delivered out of the hand of the enemy and restored to his proper place in the family.

In what way did God receive pleasure from this celebration? Because God is the God of the family and the God of order, this celebration brought Him pleasure. God's will for the family was reestablished through the dance because it was a part of the restoration process. From this example we can see that the dead things in our families can be revived, the lost things can be restored, and order can come out of chaos through the ministry of the dance.

Think on These Things

After reading *Biblical God-Inspired Dancing*, I have a
greater appreciation for . . .

_____

_____

_____

_____

_____

_____

_____

_____

_____

_____

_____

_____

_____

_____

_____

_____

_____

_____

_____

_____

_____

_____

_____

Chapter Five

Dance as Praise and Worship

"Dancing faces you towards Heaven, whichever
direction you turn."
—Terri Guillemets

As I have shared in previous chapters, dance is dear to God's heart; it brings Him delight and is used as an effective instrument in His plan for the Kingdom. Dance inspired by the Father expresses praise and the psalmist subscribes to this thought in Psalm 149:3, *"Let them praise His name in the dance . . ."* When God's name is exalted in the dance it speaks of His character, His attributes and His power. It lets us know who He is and what He is able to do as the all-powerful God.

Since God is the Creator and sustainer of all creation, all are commanded to praise Him.

Let everything that hath breath praise the LORD. Praise ye the LORD.

—Psalm 150:6

Praise the Lord!
   Praise the Lord from the heavens;
   Praise Him in the heights!
   Praise Him, all His angels;
   Praise Him, all His hosts!
   Praise Him, sun and moon;
   Praise Him, all you stars of light!
   Praise Him, you heavens of heavens,
   And you waters above the heavens!
                        —Psalm 148:1-4

Some would think that only those things that have lungs should praise God, but all creation has the breath of God. When God spoke the worlds into existence, He expelled His breath and things came into being. Therefore, because He is the Creator of all things and all things are subject to Him, it is the natural course of action for all things to praise Him. Psalm 19:1-2 states:

The heavens declare the glory of God; and the firmament sheweth His handywork. Day unto day uttereth speech, and night unto night sheweth knowledge.

Praise is giving God glory for who He is and for what He does. In doing so we magnify Him and acknowledge that He is greater than anything or any other god. The Almighty God desires our praise and He will get what He desires from all His creation. We have a choice to praise Him willingly out of a grateful heart; however, the day is coming when all will acknowledge Him.

. . . That at the name of Jesus every knee should bow, of things in heaven, and things in earth, and things under the earth: and that every tongue should confess that Jesus Christ is Lord, to the glory of God the Father.

—Philippians 2:10-11

Praise takes on many forms. We can and should praise God through vocal expression and physical actions. In doing so we should praise Him with all of our being. We praise others for jobs well done by giving them compliments, hugs and kisses, pats on the backs, citations, bonuses and gifts. If we honor vessels of clay in this manner, what greater things should we do for our Creator?

For those who say they love God, praising Him is not an option. We have been chosen to proclaim the praises of Him who called us out of darkness into the marvelous light. (See 1 Peter 2:9.)

In His Word God has commanded how He wants to be praised. We either follow His command or live in disobedience. King David was a praiser, so much so that he wrote over seventy praise songs to God. They are recorded in the Book of Psalms and there are portions in other parts of the Scriptures. David is a good example of a person who praised God even when he did not feel like it. Many people do not give God the praise that He commands because their flesh does not want to line up with the will of God. David once asked his soul, representing his mind, will and emotions,

Why art thou cast down, O my soul? And why art thou disquieted within me? Hope in God: for I shall yet praise Him, who is the health of my countenance, and my God.

—Psalm 43:5

Even though there were times when David did not feel like praising God, he knew he could not allow his soul (mind) to tell his spirit (heart) what to do. He acknowledged that the only hope he had was in lifting up the Almighty. And it is the only hope that we have.

Some Forms of Praise

In the Hebrew Scriptures, there are seven forms of praise that please God. Several were also listed in chapter two.

- **Yadah**: To revere or worship with extended hands, to throw, an expression of thanks. Extending or lifting the hands acknowledges that we are surrendering our hearts to God. It is an act of submission. We are in a position that shields us from the enemy. What can the devil do with a heart that is surrendered to God? Lifting the hands makes us only vulnerable to God. Psalm 134:2 states, *"Lift up your hands in the sanctuary, and bless the LORD."* In the following references the term praise is the Hebrew term *Yadah*: Psalm 9:1; 142:7; 67:3; 118:19.

- **Towdah**: An extension of the hands with vocal expressions of adoration and thanksgiving; specifically, a choir of worshippers, a sacrifice of praise, thanksgiving. Psalm 26:7 states, *"That I may publish with the voice of thanksgiving* [towdah]*, and tell of all thy wondrous works."* Also, Psalm 100:4 declares, *"Enter into His gates with thanksgiving* [towdah], *and into His courts with praise: be thankful unto Him, and bless His name."* In the following references the term praise is the Hebrew term *Towdah*: Psalm 50:23; Psalm 69:30; 95:2; 147:7.

- **Halal**: To be clear; to make a show, to boast; and thus to be (clamorously) foolish; to rave, to celebrate. Praise is celebrating God. Many times those who praise |halal| God look foolish. Psalm 22:22 states, *"I will declare thy name unto my brethren: in the midst of the congregation will I praise [halal] thee."* In the following references the term praise is the Hebrew term *Halal*: 1 Chronicles 23:30; Psalm 149:3; 150:1.

- **Zamar**: The idea of striking with the fingers; to touch the strings or parts of a musical instrument; to make music, accompanied by the voice; to celebrate in song and music. Psalm 57:7 states, *"My heart is fixed, O God, my heart is fixed: I will sing and give praise [zamar]."* In the following references the term praise is the Hebrew term *Zamar*: Psalm 21:13; 108:1; 138:1.

- **Tehillah:** A hymn, to laud, a celebration, praise songs of admiration. It's the required manner in which we enter into the courts of our God. *"Enter into His gates with thanksgiving, and into His courts with praise [tehillah]: be thankful unto Him, and bless His name"* Psalm 100:4. In the following references the term praise is the Hebrew term *Tehillah*: Psalm 40:3; 22:3.

- **Barak**: To bless God, to kneel or bow before Him. Barak is a humble expression of praise. We show admiration for God when we bring ourselves low before Him. Deborah and Barak lifted the following song to God, as a praise song to Him. *"Praise [barak] ye the LORD for the avenging of Israel, when the people willingly offered themselves."* Judges 5:2. In the following references the term praise is the Hebrew term *Barak*: Psalm 34:1; 146:21; Psalm 95:6; 1 Chronicles 29:20.

- **Shabach**: To address in a loud tone, to pacify, commend, glory in something. *"O praise [shabach] the LORD, all ye nations: praise him, all ye people"* Psalm 117:1. In the following references the term praise is the Hebrew term *Shabach*: Psalm 47:1; Psalm 63:3; 147:12; Isaiah 12:6.[1]

The seven aforementioned Hebrew terms should give us a better understanding of some of the forms of praise and how it requires both vocal and physical expression. Now let us look at praise more closely by examining common terminology; all of which can be extracted from the Hebrew terms discussed early.

- **Lifting the Hands**: It has been said that when we lift our hands, we slap the devil in the face. We know that lifting hands is powerful because when Moses lifted his hand with the rod of God, the Red Sea rolled back and stood up to make a safe passage for the Children of Israel. (See Exodus 14:16-23.) Also, during the battle with the Amalekites, when Moses lifted his hands the Israelites prevailed. (See Exodus 17:9-11.) There is power in a worshipper's uplifted hands. It is symbolic of surrendering our ways to God and allowing Him to fight our battles. This is why the enemy fights God's people so hard in this area. The devil will tell you that you look stupid; and he will say it is not necessary. Many think that the praise and worship leader is just trying to get them to do busy work. But it is not so! Think about it . . . if the enemy can keep us bound in pride and inhibitions in this area, he gets the victory and God loses our praise.

- **Clapping** is commanded as an expression of praise to our Almighty God. *"O clap your hands, all ye people; shout unto God with the voice of triumph"* (Psalm 47:1). Clapping hands seems to be easier for most people to do than lifting of the hands. Maybe it is because this physical act does not put one in a vulnerable position. Clapping the hands produces a sound and is usually rhythmic.

- **Marching** is a means of moving forward in orderly progression. It involves timing and synchronized movement, and is used as a weapon of spiritual warfare. The children of Israel marched by tribes as they moved from camp to camp during their wilderness wandering, thus preventing chaos (Numbers 2:9, 24). During the conquest of Jericho, God commanded Joshua and the men of war to march around the city while the priest blew their trumpets. This act of obedience resulted in the walls of Jericho falling down. (See Joshua 6:3, 4, 7, 14, 15.)

- **Kneeling and Bowing** are acts of worship and obedience. We bring ourselves low by kneeling and bowing in honor of our Maker for who He is. The psalmist invites us to worship and praise God with him: *"O come, let us worship and bow down: let us kneel before the LORD our maker. For he is our God; and we are the people of his pasture, and the sheep of his hand"* (Psalm 95:6-7).

- **Singing:** The Lord commands us to sing unto Him; it honors Him and shows forth His attributes. The sound does not have to be pleasing to the human ear, God simply said,

Make a joyful noise unto the LORD, all ye lands"
(Psalm 100:1);

Sing unto the LORD, all the earth; shew forth
from day to day his salvation. (1 Chronicles
16:23);

Sing unto the LORD, O ye saints of his, and
give thanks at the remembrance of his holiness.
(Psalm 30:4);

Sing unto the LORD; for he hath done excel-
lent things: this is known in all the earth. (Isaiah
12:5);

Speaking to yourselves in psalms and hymns and
spiritual songs, singing and making melody in
your heart to the Lord (Ephesians 5:19).

* **Playing Instruments** is powerful praise. It not only
has an effect on God and His people, but the enemy
is defeated by the sound of musical instruments.
David was such a man of praise and worship that he
personally made his own instruments and set players
over them.

Moreover four thousand were porters; and four
thousand praised the LORD with the instruments
which I made, said David, to praise therewith (1
Chronicles 23:5).

The singers went before, the players on instru-
ments followed after; among them were the dam-
sels playing with timbrels (Psalm 68:25).

Praise him with the timbrel and dance: praise him with stringed instruments and organs. Praise him upon the loud cymbals: praise him upon the high sounding cymbals. Let every thing that hath breath praise the LORD. Praise ye the LORD (Psalm 150:4-6).

- **Dancing** is the form of praise on which I want to place emphasis. This is not to imply that dance is more important than the other forms of praise, however. It is to amplify the importance of its existence in the worship experience of today. Many have ignored this form of praise in the church and in their private lives. However, along with singing, playing of instruments; kneeling and bowing; giving of thanks; and the clapping and lifting of hands, God commands that we praise Him in the dance. (See Psalm 149:3; 150:4.)

Dance as Praise is Powerful

Dance is powerful. It silences the enemy and ushers us into the presence of the Lord. As we learned in chapter two, dance takes on many forms and always involves movement.

God has put power in our feet as well as in our mouths and our hands. The gospel message can be preached through the feet: Romans 10:15b states, " *. . . as it is written, How beautiful are the feet of them that preach the gospel of peace, and bring glad tidings of good things!* " This verse is not just talking about the feet of them who preach the spoken Word, but those who use their feet to also proclaim the Good News. Many people will not be drawn to salvation through the spoken word, but the Holy Spirit can and will use the feet of the dance minister to captivate their hearts.

When the name of Jesus is lifted up in the dance, people are drawn unto Him. Yes, Jesus said, if I be lifted up from the earth, I will draw all men unto me (John 12:32). Jesus was lifted up from the earth on the cross over two thousand years ago, but He needs ministers of the dance and the preached Word to continue lifting Him up by proclaiming what God has done.

Ministering in the dance prior to the delivery of the preached Word helps to prepare the heart to receive the message. The fallow ground is broken up, and it makes the soil easier to receive the Seed, which is the Word.

Out of ignorance, many Pastors fail to recognize the significance and power of the dance ministry. They tend to relegate it to the children, to give them a part in the service. Furthermore, some pastors give their dance ministry a "little time" to show off their talent. God is not pleased with this!

Some have even noted that the ministry of song tends to prepare the atmosphere for preaching; however this is true of the dance ministry as well. If truth be told, sometimes when the dance ministry ministers before the Lord, God is finished with all that He wants to do at that particular service. However, many preachers are not sensitive enough to the Holy Spirit to recognize that God has finished and moved on. They think that their prepared message is the crème de la crème of the service.

The dance ministry deserves the same level of importance and recognition as that of the music ministry, which often precedes the sermon. Many people come to church hurting, dejected and just in need of hope. Usually no one method of lifting up the name of Jesus will reach all people. Some are touched and receive deliverance through the read word, others through music, some through preaching, and yet others through the dance. We have to be sensitive and offer food to the "whole house." God always knows what is best. He knows the heart condition and needs of all His people. I believe that is why He gave us the ways in which He wants to be praised. None of these ways are just for our private devotion. They are for corporate worship as well.

There is Power in the Feet

God anoints the feet as much as He does the hands and the mouth. The word *anoint* means to rub or smear with oil (This is further discussed in Chapter Seven, The Importance of the Anointing). The anointing gives power or ability to do the work of the Lord. It gives us the ability to do what we cannot do in our own natural strength.

When the priests, who led the procession of the crossing of the Jordan, placed their feet into the river it separated and stood up in a heap and the Children of Israel crossed over on dry ground.

> And it shall come to pass, as soon as the soles of the feet of the priests that bear the ark of the LORD, the Lord of all the earth, shall rest in the waters of Jordan, that the waters of Jordan shall be cut off from the waters that come down from above; and they shall stand upon an heap. And it came to pass, when the people removed from their tents, to pass over Jordan, and the priests bearing the ark of the covenant before the people; And as they that bare the ark were come unto Jordan, and the feet of the priests that bare the ark were dipped in the brim of the water, (for Jordan overfloweth all his banks all the time of harvest,) That the waters which came down from above stood and rose up upon an heap very far from the city Adam, that is beside Zaretan: and those that came down toward the sea of the plain, even the salt sea, failed, and were cut off: and the people passed over right against Jericho. And the priests that bare the

ark of the covenant of the LORD stood firm on dry
ground in the midst of Jordan, and all the Israelites
passed over on dry ground, until all the people were
passed clean over Jordan.

—Joshua 3:13-17

Talk about power in the feet! Yes, God put the power in
the priest's feet as they were anointed for His service. As
part of the consecration ceremony of the priests, their feet
were set apart for God's use.

And he brought the other ram, the ram of consecration: and Aaron and his sons laid their hands upon
the head of the ram. And he slew it; and Moses took
of the blood of it, and put it upon the tip of Aaron's
right ear, and upon the thumb of his right hand, and
upon the great toe of his right foot. And he brought
Aaron's sons, and Moses put of the blood upon the
tip of their right ear, and upon the thumbs of their
right hands, and upon the great toes of their right
feet: and Moses sprinkled the blood upon the altar
round about.

—Leviticus 8:22-24

Dance ministers are also God's priests. I know that this
might sound amazing to some, but it is important to realize
the significance of what we do and the position we hold. In
the Old Testament, those who were priests and Levites led
Israel in celebrating what God had done for them. As we
read earlier, many of the ceremonies held were accompanied by music, singing and dancing. Furthermore, it was the
priests and Levites who had the responsibility of worshiping
before the Lord as part of their daily duties.

In the Old Testament we see where the priests went
to God on behalf of the people. We too can go to God for

others; we can intercede on behalf of the people through the dance. Yes, we have a Great High Priest, Jesus Christ. Yet, all believers are priests. Some are set apart to do a special work, but we, who have accepted Jesus Christ, are priests who are called to worship before the Lord and are responsible for maintaining the temple (our bodies). The following Scriptures highlight this point:

> Ye also, as lively stones, are built up a spiritual house, an holy priesthood, to offer up spiritual sacrifices, acceptable to God by Jesus Christ.
> —1 Peter 2:5

> But ye are a chosen generation, a royal priesthood, an holy nation, a peculiar people; that ye should shew forth the praises of him who hath called you out of darkness into his marvellous light:
> —1 Peter 2:9

> Know ye not that ye are the temple of God, and that the Spirit of God dwelleth in you?
> —1 Corinthians 3:16

> What? Know ye not that your body is the temple of the Holy Ghost which is in you, which ye have of God, and ye are not your own?
> —1 Corinthians 6:19

The power and authority that God has given allow us to use our feet as weapons to trample the enemy.

> Every place whereon the soles of your feet shall tread shall be yours: from the wilderness and Lebanon, from the river, the river Euphrates, even unto the uttermost sea shall your coast be. There shall no man be able to

stand before you: for the LORD your God shall lay
the fear of you and the dread of you upon all the land
that ye shall *tread upon,* as he hath said unto you.
—Deuteronomy 11:24-25, emphasis added

The word *tread* in the Hebrew is *darach,* and it means
to walk, march, trample and tread. Metaphorically, it means
to crush under the feet like grapes; which means the inside
gushes out. As the Children of Israel entered into the land
God promised them, everywhere the soles of their feet
touched became their possession. The authority in their feet
commanded the land to surrender to them. Although other
nations occupied the territories at the time, the Children of
Israel treading the land, however, set off the course of action
that ensured victory over the enemy. They were able to take
claim of the lands as God promised Moses in the verses ref-
erenced above.

God reassures us throughout the Scriptures that we have
power in our feet to trample and tread upon the enemy.

Happy art thou, O Israel: who is like unto thee, O
people saved by the LORD, the shield of thy help,
and who is the sword of thy excellency! And thine
enemies shall be found liars unto thee; and thou shalt
tread upon their high places.
—Deuteronomy 33:29

Thou shalt tread upon the lion and adder: the young
lion and the dragon shalt thou trample under feet.
—Psalm 91:13

Through thee will we push down our enemies:
through thy name will we tread them under that rise
up against us.
—Psalm 44:5

Look on every one that is proud, and bring him low;
and tread down the wicked in their place.

—Job 40:12

And ye shall tread down the wicked; for they shall
be ashes under the soles of your feet in the day that I
shall do this, saith the LORD of hosts.

—Malachi 4:3

In Luke 10:19, Jesus declares, *"Behold, I give unto you
power to tread on serpents and scorpions, and over all the
power of the enemy: and nothing shall by any means hurt
you."* The word tread mentioned in this Scripture is the Greek
term *pateo*. It means a path, to trample, tread down under
foot. Is it not awesome that God would give all believers
the power to trample the enemy under foot? As we do so we
make a path in the Spirit to our destiny. What can hinder us
from going forth in the things of God once the devil has been
squashed? Nothing!

As we can see from Scripture, all believers have power
in their feet to silence the work of the enemy. Those who
have been anointed by God to minister in the dance have
been given authority to claim and reclaim territories as their
feet go forth in the dance. Can you imagine how powerful
an atmosphere there would be after the dance minister goes
forth in worship before the preached Word is delivered?

I have actually seen, with my spiritual eyes, the power
and fire of God being released through the feet of dance ministers as they ministered before the Lord. One could hear a
roaring and thumping as the dance ministers moved in the
anointing. There was such a dramatic and dynamic shift
in the atmosphere that it felt like the Holy Spirit came and
engulfed the entire sanctuary.

God intends for His people to be victorious in all areas of
life. Victory comes through many means, and for the dance

minister it can come through the use of his or her feet. God is the one Who anoints the dance minister's feet with power. That power is released for healing, deliverance, salvation and comfort. In other words yokes are broken, and something is being restored and brought back into proper alignment. It is no wonder, then, why the enemy desires to silence dance in the Church and in the Kingdom of God. Dance is spiritual warfare.

The Devastating Effects of Corrupt Dancing

Dance is powerful and pleasing to God and that is why the enemy works so hard to pervert it. Lucifer, who is now satan, boldly declared that he would be like the Most High God. Everything God has, satan has attempted to gain for himself. Since he is not able to obtain it, he has waged a campaign to pervert the dance at all levels. *Pervert* means to alter from its original course, state or purpose to a distortion or corruption of its original intent; lead someone away from what is right.

How art thou fallen from heaven, O Lucifer, son of the morning! How art thou cut down to the ground, which didst weaken the nations! For thou hast said in thine heart, I will ascend into heaven, I will exalt my throne above the stars of God: I will sit also upon the mount of the congregation, in the sides of the north: I will ascend above the heights of the clouds; I will be like the most High.

—Isaiah 14:12-14

Notice satan says five times that "I will" be like or have the things that only belong to God. He could not have the dance, but he certainly did pervert it. There are at least two instances in the Bible when dancing was grossly perverted.

It did not glorify or bring pleasure to God because it served an idolatrous and sensual purpose.

When Moses went on the Mount Sinai to receive the Ten Commandments from God, satan incited the children of Israel to dance around an idol, which means they were ascribing worth to a worthless object.

> And when the people saw that Moses delayed to come down out of the mount, the people gathered themselves together unto Aaron, and said unto him, Up, make us gods, which shall go before us; for as for this Moses, the man that brought us up out of the land of Egypt, we wot not what is become of him. And Aaron said unto them, Break off the golden earrings, which are in the ears of your wives, of your sons, and of your daughters, and bring them unto me. And all the people brake off the golden earrings which were in their ears, and brought them unto Aaron. And he received them at their hand, and fashioned it with a graving tool, after he had made it a molten calf: and they said, These be thy gods, O Israel, which brought thee up out of the land of Egypt. And when Aaron saw it, he built an altar before it; and Aaron made proclamation, and said, To morrow is a feast to the LORD. And they rose up early on the morrow, and offered burnt offerings, and brought peace offerings; and the people sat down to eat and to drink, and rose up to play. And the LORD said unto Moses, Go, get thee down; for thy people, which thou broughtest out of the land of Egypt, *have corrupted themselves*: They have turned aside quickly out of the way which I commanded them: they have made them a molten calf, and *have worshipped it*, and have sacrificed thereunto, and said, These be thy gods, O Israel, which have brought thee up out of the land of Egypt

. . .And it came to pass, as soon as he came nigh unto the camp, that he saw the calf, and *the dancing*: and Moses' anger waxed hot, and he cast the tables out of his hands, and brake them beneath the mount. And the LORD said unto Moses, I have seen this people, and, behold, it is a stiffnecked people: Now therefore let me alone, that my wrath may wax hot against them, and that I may consume them: and I will make of thee a great nation. And Moses besought the LORD his God, and said, LORD, why doth thy wrath wax hot against thy people, which thou hast brought forth out of the land of Egypt with great power, and with a mighty hand?

—Exodus 32:1-11, 19, emphasis added

What a slap in the face of the Almighty God! The children of Israel, led by Aaron, deliberately made and danced around a golden calf, exalting it as the god who had been their deliverer. How soon they forgot God's goodness to them. They disgraced the God who had been so loving and kind to bring them out of the land of Egypt where they had been serving as slaves for 400 years. He lead them safely through rugged terrain and the Red Sea, and made sure all of their needs were provided. The children of Israel had not learned to trust God despite His wondrous works on their behalf. Neither did Aaron exhibit competence as a leader. They rejected the true God and started to worship a false god through perverted dancing. They corrupted themselves with idolatrous worship, and aroused God's wrath. God would have killed the entire group if it had not been for Moses' intercession. (See Exodus 32:9-14.)

Another instance of perverted dancing can be found in the New Testament. Matthew and Mark record the story.

And when a convenient day was come, that Herod on his birthday made a supper to his lords, high captains, and chief estates of Galilee; And when the daughter of the said Herodias came in, *and danced*, and pleased Herod and them that sat with him, the king said unto the damsel, Ask of me whatsoever thou wilt, and I will give it thee. And he sware unto her, Whatsoever thou shalt ask of me, I will give it thee, unto the half of my kingdom. And she went forth, and said unto her mother, What shall I ask? And she said, the head of John the Baptist.
—Mark 6:21-24, emphasis added

This is a good example of sensual or carnal dancing. Herodias' daughter performed a lustful—"dirty"—dance at Herod's birthday party. After Herodias daughter pleased Herod's fleshly desires through the dance, he granted her a wish up to one-half of his kingdom. Most people would have requested riches, fame and possibly half the kingdom. However, the most unusual request was made.

Herodias had a grudge against John the Baptist because he spoke out about the unholy relationship she had with Herod. This was an opportunity for Herodias to get even, and so she encouraged her daughter to ask for the head of John the Baptist. Herod was so moved by this perverted dance that he had John the Baptist's head delivered on a platter. This dance was so perverted that it had a strong influence over sound judgment.

As we can surmise from the two examples, perverted dancing can have powerful negative effects. Anything that belongs to God, when placed in the hands of the enemy, can have devastating consequences. Three thousand men lost their lives because of the incident with the golden calf; and the entire nation of Israel could have been wiped out as a means to appease God's wrath. John the Baptist, a holy prophet of God, was beheaded as a result of Herodias daughter's sensual dance.

As it has been discussed previously, dance is a weapon in God's arsenal. This precious gift that God has given us can be used to edify or bring destruction, depending on its purpose.

Other Forms of Dance

Prophetic dance is hearing, seeing and expressing the mind of God. When we consider the term prophesy we know it to mean foretelling; expressing the desires of God, giving encouragement, edifying and bringing comfort. Just as ministers are able to speak, preach, teach and sing prophetically through these means, dance can also be ministered prophetically. God reveals His heart to His servant and he or she vocally expresses what God reveals. In the case of dance, God shows or speaks a pattern of movement and the dance minister moves accordingly. Usually, the dance is not rehearsed or choreographed. God's message flows spontaneously unhindered by human mindset. For example, when Miriam and the women took up their tambourines and danced after the Red Sea experience, they had not rehearsed, choreographed or thought about what they would do to give praise and thanksgiving to God. They were excited about their victory over the enemy. This was spontaneous, unhindered, prophetic dance.

Warfare Dance is an aggressive dance, waging war against the enemy. It can be very demonstrative such as marching, trampling, kicking, stomping and punching. We are to crush the enemy under our feet. According to Psalm 149, dance is a weapon of warfare.

Let them praise his name in the dance: let them sing praises unto him with the timbrel and harp.

For the LORD taketh pleasure in his people: he will beautify the meek with salvation. Let the saints be joyful in glory: let them sing aloud upon their beds. Let the high praises of God be in their mouth, and a twoedged sword in their hand; To execute vengeance upon the heathen, and punishments upon the people; *To bind their kings with chains*, and their nobles with fetters of iron; To execute upon them the judgment written: this honour have all his saints. Praise ye the LORD.

vv. 3-9, emphasis added

Warfare dance binds the enemy, thwarting and frustrating his plans as breakthroughs are made by faith in the heavenlies. This type of dance is even more effective when accompanied by singing, musical instruments, and instruments of warfare: banners, flags, streamers, tambourines and praise signals. When King Jehoshaphat won the battle against the three armies that came up against Judah, he did not use physical weapons to fight the enemy. Instead, he did as God instructed, and sent the singers and praisers out before the army. God set ambush against the enemy, and Israel was able to collect the booty left by the dead armies. (See 2 Chronicles 20:21-22.)

For though we walk in the flesh, we do not war after the flesh: (For the weapons of our warfare are not carnal, but mighty through God to the pulling down of strong holds;)

—2 Corinthians 10:3-4

As you have discovered, the dance is tremendously powerful, it arouses the flesh, soul and spirit. In light of this, it is important for us to minister as unto the Lord, moving by the leading of the Spirit as He fills us with His presence. Spirit-filled dance is a sure defense against the enemy's influence. Satan, our archenemy, has accelerated his attacks against the purity of the dance, as he is aware that God is restoring it for its original purpose—to bring pleasure and glory to His name.

Think On These Things

After reading *Dance as Praise and Worship*, I have
become more aware of . . .

_____

_____

_____

_____

_____

_____

_____

_____

_____

_____

_____

_____

_____

_____

_____

_____

_____

_____

_____

_____

_____

_____

_____

Chapter Six

The Dance is Being Restored

*"Nobody cares if you can't dance well. Just get up
and dance."*
—Dave Barry

W hen the Holy spirit moved upon the face of the
waters during creation, the dance was pure and powerful, uninhibited by human or demonic interferences and
constraints. Therefore, God's will and purpose for the dance
was accomplished. A beautiful and orderly world emerged
out of what was once a mass of chaos. Over the course of
time, however, dance has been corrupted and perverted; it
has practically lost its original purpose—to bring pleasure to
God and to restore order. According to Acts 3:21, there is a
time of restoration of all things.

> And he shall send Jesus Christ, which before was
> preached unto you: Whom the heaven must receive
> until the times of *restitution* of all things, which God
> hath spoken by the mouth of all his holy prophets
> since the world began.
>
> —3:20-21, emphasis added

The word *restitution* is *apokatastasis* in the Greek language. It means restoration; of the perfect state before the Fall. Peter is speaking of a time when everything God created will be refreshed and returned to its original state.

What is Restoration?

To *restore* means to make whole again. Something that was broken, shattered, corrupted, wounded, hurt or bruised is returned to its original condition. The world and everything in it has been broken and corrupted by sin.

> For the creature was made subject to vanity, not willingly, but by reason of him who hath subjected the same in hope, Because the creature itself also shall be delivered from the bondage of corruption into the glorious liberty of the children of God. For we know that the whole creation groaneth and travaileth in pain together until now.
>
> —Romans 8:20-21

> For all have sinned, and come short of the glory of God.
>
> —Romans 3:23

God's intent has always been restoration. The first promise of restoration can be found in Genesis 3:15.

> And I will put enmity between thee and the woman, and between thy seed and her seed; it shall bruise thy head, and thou shalt bruise his heel.

God is speaking of a time when the source of corruption—satan, our adversary—would be overthrown and a state of righteousness would be restored in the earth. Since we are approaching the return of Christ, it appears that God has accelerated the process of restoration. He is retrieving what the enemy has corrupted and perverted, and returning it to its original state and purpose.

Restoration: God's Plan

The fall of man and the subsequent corruption of the earth were no surprise to God because He foreknew the power of His creation. As is natural to God and His creation, there is the capacity for restoration as within each created thing there is life within itself. For example, in Genesis 1:11-12, 21-22, 26-28, God brought into existence plant life, animals and humankind that had seed within itself (the ability to regenerate its likeness).

Likewise, when His chosen people, Israel, strayed and chose to worship idol gods, God could not allow them to go their own way. He warned them repeatedly to put away their idols and return to Him or else He would intervene with judgment. Sadly, they did not listen to their Creator and were surely punished. God allowed foreign nations to overrun them and force them into exile. Nevertheless, God was merciful. Before the Babylonians took them away, God gave them hope of restoration. He told Jeremiah to tell His people that a remnant would be saved.

> For thus saith the LORD, that after seventy years be accomplished at Babylon I will visit you, and perform my good word toward you, in causing you to return to this place. For I know the thoughts that I think toward you, saith the LORD, thoughts of peace, and not of evil, to give you an expected end.
> —Jeremiah 29:10-11

God promised that even though Israel would experience some dark and sad days due to their own rebellion, in due time their joy and gladness would be restored.

> Again I will build thee, and thou shalt be built, O virgin of Israel: thou shalt again be adorned with thy tabrets, and shalt go forth in the dances of them that make merry. . .Then shall the virgin *rejoice in the dance*, both young men and old together: for I will turn their mourning into joy, and will comfort them, and make them rejoice from their sorrow.
> —Jeremiah 31:4, 13, emphasis added

As we mentioned earlier, within restoration there is hope. Job speaks emphatically about this when he describes the hopeless state of a tree.

> For there is hope of a tree, if it be cut down, that it will sprout again, and that the tender branch thereof will not cease. Though the root thereof wax old in the earth, and the stock thereof die in the ground; Yet through the scent of water it will bud, and bring forth boughs like a plant.
> —Job 14:7-9

On the surface the tree appeared to be dead, lifeless, without any hope of restoration. The root and the stump remained old for some time; however, just the scent of water would give it hope, revitalization, an extension on life and the ability to bud again.

As with the tree's outward looking demise, so with the perversion and corruption of the dance. Though there has been a plot by the devil to bring corruption to the purity of the dance, there is hope. Why, you may be asking? As with the creation of seed bearing plants, animals and humankind, so it is with the ministry of the dance because God had already devised the plan for its restoration. In Acts 3:20-21, the time of restitution has come for the dance. God has breathed new life; fresh breath on it, and the dance is coming to life again. The aroma of God is being sensed throughout the earth, awakening those who God has foreordained to carry the anointing of the dance. Life is coming back to what God created to bring Him pleasure and order in the earth.

God sees dancing as a part of and as evidence of restoration. When we are able to truly rejoice and make merry from the depth of our being, it is proof that all sadness, grief, despondency and apathy toward the dance have been eradicated. God's promise to the returning exiles was that He would inspire them to dance in the same manner that He inspired Miriam and the women to dance during the great Exodus from Egypt.

Dance has always been a part of God's plan. It gives Him pleasure and it has restorative benefits for the dancer and the audience as well. Through King David, God commands His people to dance, *"Let them praise His name in the dance: let them sing praises unto Him with the timbrel and harp . . . Praise Him with the timbrel and dance: praise Him with stringed instruments and organs"* Psalm 149:3; 150:4. Today, God is restoring the dance in the manner that David knew it—from the heart, pure and holy, God-centered, victorious, celebratory, thankful, and joyous.

Proper Restoration

Sometime ago when God was dealing with me concerning my apostolic calling, He prompted me to read Jeremiah 1:10 everyday for about a month. It reads:

See, I have this day set thee over the nations and over the kingdoms, to root out, and to pull down, and to destroy, and to throw down, to build, and to plant.

God, through this verse of Scripture, was showing me the process of restoration. Before there can be building and planting, there has to be a rooting out, pulling down, destroying and throwing down of the old; the old mindsets, old habits, old traditions and old methodologies. Rooting out is vital because all things of the old must go. If any part of it were to remain, there is a good chance that it will sprout again. Destruction and annihilation are necessary no matter the cost. In Scripture, we find where God commanded Israel to kill its enemies, even the women and babies. The babies carried the same blood DNA as their parents. The possibility existed that they would grow up and become a terror to Israel.

Now go and smite Amalek, and utterly destroy all that they have, and spare them not; but slay both man and woman, infant and suckling, ox and sheep, camel and ass.
—1 Samuel 15:3

For example, when old buildings are being restored, all later additions must be stripped away and the building returned to its original condition. For example, if a 19th century church is being restored after it was modernized with 20th century stain glass windows, the 20th century windows would have to be removed and replaced with 19th century windows. Furthermore, if the original wood exterior of the church building has been updated to aluminum siding, the siding must be removed and the wood painted its original paint type and color. In other words, in restoration, everything must return to the original condition.

In the natural, all things cannot be restored. For example, all buildings cannot be restored because of changes in ordinances, construction laws or the availability of materials. In some cases, some buildings are allowed to be preserved as historical buildings; however, there is a difference in preservation and restoration.

In the spirit realm, however, all things can and will be restored that was spoken of by the mouth of the holy prophets. God's original intent for all things will come back into alignment. Let me state what this does not mean. It does not mean that everything will look and sound like it did in the past. However, the spiritual power and purpose of all things will be what God intended it to be from the beginning. For example, there was a time when God commanded His people to worship Him at a certain place, at a certain time, using a specific method. When Jesus came on the scene, He declared, you will still worship my Father, however, not at a specified place, time or method. All true worshippers will worship the Father in spirit and in truth, anytime, and anywhere. (See John 4:23-24.) The spirit of worship remained the same, but the form and method of worship began to change. Worship would no longer be legalistic and ritualistic.

Restoration does not mean that we will return to the practice of keeping the law or legalism. Rather, the spiritual power and purposes behind these laws will be restored. A good example of this is partaking of communion or the Lord's Supper. When our Lord established communion on the night that He was betrayed in Jerusalem, the twelve disciples sat with Him at the table. They ate from one loaf and drank from one cup. Today most of us attend churches where the communion trays are passed from one person to another; and we do not sit at a table. The elements or sacraments (the fruit of the vine and the bread) are packaged in a small plastic container. The method has changed for most of us, but the spirit of communion remains the same.

During the renewal process there must be a "rooting out and tearing down." Rooting out and tearing down can be and usually is an uncomfortable process. Imagine a plant being pulled up from the only soil that it has known; it has been settled in this soil for many years. The pulling and tugging will cause some tension, resistance and maybe some shock. Likewise, when our mind is being reworked there will be some tension, resistance, and perhaps disturbed surprise. More than likely the old thoughts, understandings, revelations and ideals will initially resist the restoration process. This is natural and normal. However, we cannot allow the discomfort to cause us to abort the new understanding, especially when the old is erroneous, obsolete or limited in scope. For example, I was reared from a child to believe that I could lose my salvation. Therefore, I did not have the joy of my salvation because I was literally being tormented with the thoughts of possibly going to hell if my behavior was not holy. I was led to believe that living a holy life or a life pleasing to God was centered on outward appearances and behaviors. I was taught that wearing pants, make-up, jewelry and sandals were taboo. Going to the movies, ball games, parties and playing with dice would certainly make God angry. On the other hand, wearing long colorless dresses, stockings and sporting "nappy" unpressed hair brought God pleasure. This is just a partial list of the do's and don't that I was taught to believe would be pleasing to God because it was considered holy.

In my early adulthood I went on a quest for truth. I wanted to know why I was saved (born again), but was so miserable? Subsequently, God directed me to a traditional Baptist church where I was taught the truth concerning salvation and eternal security. When the Scriptures were first explained to me regarding these subjects, my natural mind resisted it initially. I could not grasp what was being taught because my old mindset had become rigid and rooted in legalism. I tried to rationalize with my mind how these things could be true. The following are some of the Scriptures that were taught to me:

> For the gifts and calling of God are without repentance.
>
> —Romans 11:29

> For by grace are ye saved through faith; and that not of yourselves: it is the gift of God: Not of works, lest any man should boast.
>
> —Ephesians 2:8-9

> Which is the earnest of our inheritance until the redemption of the purchased possession, unto the praise of his glory.
>
> —Ephesians 1:14

> And grieve not the Holy Spirit of God, whereby ye are sealed unto the day of redemption.
>
> —Ephesians 4:30

> Being confident of this very thing, that he which hath begun a good work in you will perform it until the day of Jesus Christ.
>
> —Philippians 1:6

These Scriptures assure us of our position in Christ, which cannot be changed or altered. Salvation is a free gift of God that cannot be revoked. The moment a person places saving faith in Jesus Christ, the Holy Spirit indwells and seals him/her until the day of redemption. Praise the Lord!

Upon entering seminary, I was not fully persuaded of the truth regarding salvation as it related to eternal security; however, as I continued to study the Scriptures, gradually the

Word regenerated my mind. The walls of rationalization were being torn down, and over time my mind was totally renewed by the washing of the Word. Yes, it took a few years of rooting out and tearing down of old mindsets through diligent study and desire for truth and transformation to take place. I am no longer held in bondage by legalistic and religious thinking regarding the doctrine of salvation. Thanks be to God for giving me the grace to walk through this process and not allowing the initial discomfort to cause me to abort the truth.

Many times we may be hesitant and feel uncomfortable about receiving new revelation when it is presented because it seems that we are betraying the persons who initially taught us. I do understand this rational, as this was one of my concerns. Nevertheless, we must realize that our loved ones can only teach to the measure of their understanding. They do not deliberately lead us on a wrong path.

The process of renewing the mind, which brings restoration, is also uncomfortable because it stretches us. We have to get out of our comfort zones and dive into uncharted waters. Many want God to enlarge their territory while they hold on to old mindsets. It will not happen. God must be given the freedom to strip away the old to make way for the new. He said putting new wine in old wine skins would cause the old skins to break and the new wine would run out. (See Matthew 9:17.) The following Scriptures command us to renew the mind.

> And be not conformed to this world: but be ye transformed by the renewing of your mind, that ye may prove what is that good, and acceptable, and perfect, will of God.
>
> —Romans 12:2

> And be renewed in the spirit of your mind.
>
> —Ephesians 4:23

And have put on the new man, which is renewed in knowledge after the image of him that created him:
—Colossians 3:10

We cannot see from God's perspective until our minds are renewed. The word renewing is the Greek term *anakainosis*; it comes from a combination of two words: *ana* meaning "again" and *kainos* which means "new." *Anakainosis* means to cause to grow up, to make new, to be changed into a new kind of life as oppose to the former corrupt state. It implies a restoration of moral and spiritual vision. Whenever new revelation or understanding is being presented to us, we should not be quick to discard or label it as false doctrine. We should do like the Bereans who searched the Scriptures to see if the things taught were true.

These [Bereans] were more noble than those in Thessalonica, in that they received the word with all readiness of mind, and searched the scriptures daily, whether those things were so.
—Acts 17:11

We must allow God to wash us with the washing of His Word. The Word will wash away the pollutants—that which we have been taught in error by the world, our own intellect and even the church. After which, we should ask God to open the eyes of our understanding so that we can see from His perspective.

Open thou mine eyes, that I may behold wondrous things out of thy law.
—Psalm 119:18

Go to God like a newborn baby and ask God to teach you from the "ground up." That is exactly what I did. I said,

"Lord, strip me of everything I was taught in error and start over with me." I had to release myself to God and trust that He would give me proper guidance. It is not until we turn the reigns of our mind over to God that He can start the restoration process: rooting out, pulling down, destroying, building and planting.

Getting to the Root

In order to understand dance as God originally intended, we must get to the root, that is we must gain an understanding of the Hebrew culture since God gave the dance to the Jew first.

. . .To the Jew first, and also to the Greek.
—Romans 1:16b

Everything that God gave to build His Kingdom in the earth, He gave to the Jew first, and praise and worship dance is no exception. Salvation and the knowledge of the true and living God came to the Jew first. The gift of the Holy Spirit was given to the Jews assembled in the Upper Room in Jerusalem. There were no Gentiles among the one hundred and twenty souls gathered.

When anything is severed from its root system, if it does not die altogether, it will lose its originality and become detached and isolated. No longer associated or attached to the original (root), it takes on a life of its own and is influenced by its surroundings. Since the first group of people to whom God gave the dance were Jews; praise and worship dance is therefore rooted in Judaism. In order for us (New Testament) believers to bring pleasure to God in the dance, we must gain an understanding of, appreciation for, and incorporate Hebraic customs and culture in our dance.

We, the Gentiles, were engrafted (adopted into the body of Christ) and are now spiritual Jews or Jews by faith.

And if ye be Christ's, then are ye Abraham's seed, and heirs according to the promise.
—Galatians 3:29

Wherefore remember, that ye being in time past Gentiles in the flesh, who are called Uncircumcision by that which is called the Circumcision in the flesh made by hands; That at that time ye were without Christ, being aliens from the commonwealth of Israel, and strangers from the covenants of promise, having no hope, and without God in the world: But now in Christ Jesus ye who sometimes were far off are made nigh by the blood of Christ.
—Ephesians 2:11-13

The Jewish people incorporated dance in all their festivities; marriages, feasts, births, etc. God established feast days that He commanded the Jews to observe with rejoicing. Their lives revolved around dancing and making merry. God does not require us to observe the ritualistic keeping of the feast days, however, we should be aware of them and how it connects to Christ and the impact they have on natural-born Jews.

As we know, King David was a worshipper as was discussed before. He went beyond the ritualism of worship established by Moses and replaced it with a new spiritual order of worship where God was ministered to 24 hours a day through singing, dancing, clapping, shouting, rejoicing, thanking, recording, lifting the hands, seeking the Lord and playing of instruments. (See 1 Chronicles 15-17.)

Though the tabernacle of David has fallen due to Israel's disobedience, God promises to raise it up again.

> In that day will I raise up the tabernacle of David that
> is fallen, and close up the breaches thereof; and I will
> raise up his ruins, and I will build it as in the days of
> old . . .
>
> —Amos 9:11

God is restoring the tabernacle of David because it
serves as a model for spiritual worship and Christian practice. The dancing associated with David's tabernacle was
certainly Jewish. If we are going to be a part of what God is
doing in this hour, we must get an understanding of Jewish
dancing. The restoring of David's tabernacle is preparation
for Christ's return. Christ's return will be accompanied by
joy and gladness.

> And I heard as it were the voice of a great multitude,
> and as the voice of many waters, and as the voice
> of mighty thunderings, saying, Alleluia: for the Lord
> God omnipotent reigneth. Let us be *glad* and *rejoice*,
> and give honour to him: for the marriage of the Lamb
> is come, and his wife hath made herself ready.
>
> —Revelation 19:6-7, emphasis added.

At the marriage supper of the Lamb, there will be singing,
dancing and praising of our King. Since Jesus was born
a Jew, more than likely the dancing will be of the Jewish
origin. As ministers of the dance, we are going to be a part
of the festivities, and we need to learn the Jewish style of
dancing. God made and appreciates all nations, and they will
be represented around His throne.

> After this I beheld, and, lo, a great multitude, which
> no man could number, of all nations, and kindreds,
> and people, and tongues, stood before the throne,

and before the Lamb, clothed with white robes, and
palms in their hands; ...

— Revelation 7:9

It is therefore, to our advantage to learn about the Hebraic
root of dance, and appreciate what God is doing in the earth
with the restoration of the dance.

Think On These Things

After reading *The Dance is Being Restored*, I am excited
about . . .

_____

_____

_____

_____

_____

_____

_____

_____

_____

_____

_____

_____

_____

_____

_____

_____

_____

_____

_____

_____

_____

_____

_____

_____

Chapter Seven

The Dance Minister

*"Dance is the only art of which we ourselves are the
stuff of which it is made."*
—Ted Shawn

The first question that needs to be settled in the mind
of the dancer is; have I received a call from God to
minister in the dance before Him and His people? This is a
major concern, since the church in so many people's minds
is just a Sunday morning club. Many, including some pastors, do not concern themselves with whether an individual
has a call on his or her life to minister in the dance. There are
also those who are ignorant to the importance and purpose
of the dance. And as a result, greater works are not being
accomplished. God declares, *"My people are destroyed for
lack of knowledge"* (Hosea 4:6a).

Because dance is up front and "showy," so to speak, some
people desire to be a part of the dance ministry. Our techno-
logical age has created a desire in many to be Hollywood
stars and entertainers. The proof of this is evident in the rise
and popularity of reality shows on television and it appears
that the need for popularity is sneaking into the church.

The worship service is not a time of entertainment. God did not call us to be superstars; He is the only One who should be the center of attention during worship. Yes, it is great when we can laugh and have fun during the worship service. God permits it and informs us that laughter is like good medicine; it brings healing to the soul. Dancing before the Lord, however, is not performance. It is ministry! Most people who come to church are broken, hurting, bereaved and downcast, and only ministry can meet the need of their situation. It is during that time that God pours out His healing balm to soothe doubts, calm fears and heal the aching heart. On the other hand, entertainment is a quick fix that will not endure the test of time.

The ministry of dance is just as serious as ministering the Spoken Word and should be taken as such. It may appear that I am saying that dance is reserved for a sacred few, but that is not the case. Everyone can and should praise God in the dance. At times, the whole congregation should dance in the worship service. Sometimes there are moves of God, when the entire congregation will burst out in beautiful praise unto God in the dance; however, this is not the order for every service.

God does call and appoint some to the ministry of dance. They have been empowered by God to usher in His presence and to release a particular anointing in the atmosphere. A call goes beyond a mere desire; it is a passion, a driving impulse. When a call is not fulfilled, there is a void and a sense of restlessness.

That is why God told Paul, that it is hard for him to kick against the pricks. (See Acts 9:5.) The "pricks" is also translated "goad." A goad is a sharp instrument used to drive cattle by inflicting pain. So a prick is a driving, divine impulse. This prick would cause the cattle to get moving and to move in a desired direction. The Lord was saying to Paul, it's hard to fight against a divine dream or assignment. Fighting against a divine call can cause us to engage in useless and dangerous pursuits the way Paul did. Instead of ministering life to God's people (his assignment), he was killing them. (See Acts 7:58, 9:1.)

How Do You Know If You Have Been Called?

One of the ways we receive a divine call is through a conviction in our spirit. A conviction is a firm belief or persuasion; it is a sensing in our spirit; or a witness in the heart that God has ordained us to do a particular work—in this case dance. Sometimes we are also convinced that God has called us to do so by our active engagement in the dance. In essence, "Just Try It" and see if this is a ministry God has called you to. If such is the case, others around you will see it as well, including your leaders. As I mentioned in the introduction, it was through one of these means that I received my call to the dance ministry.

The call also comes with spiritual equipping. God equips those He calls and gives us the gift or skill to do ministry; however, it is up to us to perfect it. We need to be convinced ourselves that God has called us. Do not become a part of a dance ministry or any other ministry, if you are not persuaded that God called you to it. Many times people, even our parents, will try to persuade us to become a dance minister because of their own selfishness or lack of knowledge, but I encourage you to seek God's will.

Character Expectations Of Those Called of God

As we discussed previously, there is an anointing and call on one's life to minister before the Lord and His people. With the call comes certain expectations that we have to exhibit in our life to be effective ministers of the dance. Because God is using the dance to help restore the tabernacle of David and to usher in Christ's return, there has to be a lifestyle of purity, intimacy, commitment, discipline, flexibility and sensitivity to God's leading. The following are some character expectations that should be exhibited in the life of one who has been called and is operating in ministry. We know that character is developed over time, therefore, please understand that the same is true of the following expectations.

Realize the seriousness of the call.

Generally, when we realize how serious it is to minister unto God and before His people, we don't typically run to the call. We may take our time and weigh the matter, however we are not alone in this response. The Bible has examples of those who responded to their call in different ways.

- Moses was called to lead the children of Israel out of Egypt, but he thought of his limitations and the responsibilities. He made excuses, grumbled and hesitated so long God became angry with him. (See Exodus 3-4.)

- Jeremiah took his call as a prophet of God very seriously and He gave God some "back talk" before he accepted his assignment. (See Jeremiah 1.)

- Jonah received his call from God but ran away from the responsibility. Instead of going to Nineveh and preaching to the people, warning them of impending doom if they did not change their ways; he boarded a ship to Tarnish, which went in the opposite direction of where he was supposed to be going. (See Jonah 1-3.)

- Gideon, the sixth Judge of Israel, was called to lead a mighty army and to defeat the enemies of God's people; however, he was not receptive to the call because he responded out of his insecurity. When God called him to rule over Israel, He addressed him as "a mighty man of valor." However, Gideon did not take note of the empowerment of the salutation; instead, He questioned the power, presence and promises of God to Israel. In addition, in order to go forth with the mandate God gave him, he needed documented proof that God would use him to bring deliverance to Israel. (See Judges 6.)

- Paul (formerly known as Saul) was called to the ministry of the gospel in a dramatic fashion. He was affected physically and emotionally as his first encounter with God came with bright lights, loud noise, blindness, isolation and hunger. There was no doubt that God had called him. Ananias, a devout disciple of Jesus Christ who feared Saul, the chief persecutor of the brethren, confirmed Paul's divine encounter with God. Although Paul's call was so dramatic, and he began this new ministry with such intense passion and with obvious success, he thought himself unworthy to be considered an apostle of Jesus Christ. His past actions weighed in heavily upon his perception of himself although God had called him to such a great ministry. (See Acts 9:1-22; 1 Corinthians 15:1-11; 1 Timothy 1:12-13.)

- Mary was chosen of God with the awesome responsibility to give birth and nurture God's only Son, Jesus Christ. The announcement of the news startled Mary and she questioned how this would be as she was a virgin espoused to another man. She questioned and pondered the matter in her heart before she responded, *"Be it unto me according to thy word!"* (See Luke 1:28-38.)

Ask any preacher of today and they will more than likely have the testimony that they ran or hesitated before accepting their assignment. And I am no exception, because I ran for many years before I said yes to God. I basically took the time and weighed the seriousness of the assignment. Ministry in any form is serious business and should be taken as such. Anyone who has a call from God will have a consciousness of the great responsibility of the assignment and will consider it before making a commitment.

Submit to authority.

God regards authority very seriously. We can see evidences of this throughout Scripture when He judged those who rebelled against established authority. Paul emphatically proclaims in Romans 13:1 that all authority is of God; therefore, we should submit ourselves to the governing authorities. For the dance minister this would include leadership in the church: Apostle, Pastor and Dance Ministry Director. However, this does not preclude any other leadership who has authority over the dance ministry. When a dance minister is not submitted to leadership he or she is in rebellion causing his or her ministry to be ineffective. The subject of submission is elaborated on in chapter eight, Me, A Servant.

Discipline to grow spiritually.

God requires us to make progress in our spiritual life, so He has equipped us with the necessary grace to discipline ourselves spiritually and to foster intimacy with Him. Prayer, fasting and study of His Word are key components for growth. Jesus realized the importance of prayer and took the time to teach His disciples to pray. Prayer is an open line of communication between us and the Father through Jesus

Christ. There were times when Jesus took the time to go off to pray to the Father even as the Son of God.

Fasting is not only beneficial to our physical body but also is important in building our spirit man. (See Isaiah 58.) The discipline of fasting also helps us be more sensitive to God and de-clutters the mind so that we can draw closer to Him.

In Second Timothy 2:15, Paul states, *"Study to shew thyself approved unto God, a workman that needeth not to be ashamed, rightly dividing the word of truth."* If we are going to minister the Word through music/song and dance then we need to know the Word. Dance ministers should be students of the Word. And, according to Paul, our study should be to God's satisfaction or approval. One should study their craft. Yes, those who are called are anointed, but the question to be considered is, "Is the anointing enough?" The anointing is enabling power; it enhances the gift or skill. What's more important is character. Character is one's mental and moral qualities or reputation. The anointing coupled with good character makes one's ministry effective. One is as important as the other. Think of it this way, the anointing is the door opener and character is the door-jam.

Have a teachable spirit.

Those of us who God has called, appointed and anointed to the ministry of dance should never think that we know it all. Even if we have studied dance professionally and have seen God use us in the dance to transform the lives of multitudes, we still do not possess all there is to know about dance and the worship arts. There should be a willingness to receive from others. There is yet much to be learned. God is not interested in professionalism and correct technique as much as He is in submission and obedience. He can and does use simple, unrehearsed, unskilled movement to bless His people. When we hear from God and move accordingly, we bring glory to His name. According to 1 Corinthians 1:27-29, God purposely uses the foolish and base things of the world to put the wise to shame and to bring glory to His name.

Having a teachable spirit requires that we remain humble and open to new ideas and methods of ministry. When we have and cultivate a teachable spirit we leave no room for pride to take root in our hearts. Pride is an exaggerated opinion of ourselves; an exalted attitude. According to Proverbs 16:18, *"Pride goeth before destruction, and a haughty spirit before a fall."* The consequences of walking in pride is evident in the following Scriptures:

> All this came upon the king Nebuchadnezzar. At the end of twelve months he walked in the palace of the kingdom of Babylon. The king spake, and said, Is not this great Babylon, that I have built for the house of the kingdom by the might of my power, and for the honour of my majesty? While the word was in the king's mouth, there fell a voice from heaven, saying, O king Nebuchadnezzar, to thee it is spoken; The kingdom is departed from thee.
>
> —Daniel 4:28-31

> But when his heart was lifted up, and his mind hardened in pride, he was deposed from his kingly throne, and they took his glory from him: And he was driven from the sons of men; and his heart was made like the beasts, and his dwelling was with the wild asses: they fed him with grass like oxen, and his body was wet with the dew of heaven; till he knew that the most high God ruled in the kingdom of men, and that he appointeth over it whomsoever he will. And thou his son, O Belshazzar, hast not humbled thine heart, though thou knewest all this; But hast lifted

up thyself against the Lord of heaven; and they have brought the vessels of his house before thee, and thou, and thy lords, thy wives, and thy concubines, have drunk wine in them; and thou hast praised the gods of silver, and gold, of brass, iron, wood, and stone, which see not, nor hear, nor know: and the God in whose hand thy breath is, and whose are all thy ways, hast thou not glorified.

—Daniel 5:20-23

And upon a set day Herod, arrayed in royal apparel, sat upon his throne, and made an oration unto them. And the people gave a shout, saying, It is the voice of a god, and not of a man. And immediately the angel of the Lord smote him, because he gave not God the glory: and he was eaten of worms, and gave up the ghost.

—Acts 5:21-23

Nebuchadnezzar and Herod (leaders of great empires) were not aware that God took note of their actions. Both thought and spoke in pride and arrogance, and did not give God the glory by submitting their accomplishments to the Creator of all things. God had to remind them through judgment of who they were and who He is. According to Proverbs 29:23, *One's pride will bring him low, but he who is lowly in spirit will obtain honor.* As we can see, pride can have a devastating effect on our lives and ministries. Our purpose is to bring honor and glory to God, and we can do so by nurturing a teachable spirit before Him. Pride should have no place in what we do for the Father because He rewards those who walk in humility. Are you looking for a reward? I am!

Receive correction.

We who possess a teachable spirit will receive correction. We live in a rebellious era and most people do not want to be corrected or receive wise counsel. The days that we are living in are very similar to the days the Judges ruled in Israel, *"every man did that which was right in his own eyes."* (Judges 21:25b) Defying correction and counsel is unwise according to the Word of God. Proverbs, the book of Wisdom, states; *"where no counsel is, the people fall . . ."* *"The way of a fool is right in his own eyes: but he that hearkeneth unto counsel is wise." "Hear counsel, and receive instruction, that thou mayest be wise in they latter end."* *" . . . And in multitude of counselors there is safety"* (11:14; 12:15; 19:20; 24:6b).

Those of us who minister before the Lord must have and retain a posture to receive correction. Again, ministering before God and His people is serious business. He cannot be glorified through a rebellious, "do it my own way" heart. God places pastors, mentors, teachers, counselors, and parents in our life to correct and show us how to please Him. God takes the matter of rebellion very seriously. He literally banished Lucifer, now satan, and all the angels who conspired with him, out of heaven due to rebellion.

When Korah and company rose up against Moses in the wilderness, God dealt with them harshly. God did something that had never been done before. He opened up the earth underneath them and they and their possessions were swallowed alive.

> But if the Lord make a new thing, and the earth opens her mouth and, swallow them up, with all that appertain unto them, and they go down quick into the pit; then ye shall understand that these men have provoked [rejected] the Lord. And it came to pass, as he had made an end of speaking all these words, that

the ground clave a sunder [split apart] that was under them, and the earth opened its mouth and swallowed them up, with their households and all the men with Korah, with all their goods. So they and all those with them went down alive into the pit; the earth closed over them, and they perished from among the assembly.

—Numbers 16:30-33

Most of the children of Israel, who suffered in Egypt, never got to see the Promised Land because of their rebellion and constant complaining. (See Numbers 14:26-35.) When we rebel, we become our own counselor and we listen to our own heart. However, in doing so, we run the risk of going astray and doing things contrary to the will of God. Jeremiah 17:9 states, *"The heart is deceitful above all things, and desperately wicked: who can know it?"* We do not know our own heart and therefore our heart will deceive us.

When we choose not to be open to receive correction, it is because we have decided to give in to the spirit of haughtiness (pride), which manifests itself through the following:

- **Rebellion** means to oppose authority or resist established order. This is what God has to say about rebellion in I Samuel 15:23, *"For rebellion is as the sin of witchcraft, and stubbornness is as iniquity and idolatry. Because thou hast rejected the word of the LORD, he hath also rejected thee from being king."*

- **Conspiracy** goes beyond mere rebellion; it happens when a group of rebellious people gets together to agree to overthrow or resist authority, such was the case with Korah and company. Joseph's brothers conspired to kill him (See Genesis 37:18-20.); Miriam and Aaron conspired against Moses (See Numbers

12; 14:4; 16:1-35.); and the Pharisees plotted to kill Jesus (See Matthew 12:14.).

- **Mutiny** is another term for rebellion; it can be passive or aggressive. Korah and company is a good example of aggressive mutiny, *"And they said one to another, Let us make a captain, and let us return into Egypt"* (See Numbers 14:4.). Passive mutiny is working in secrecy to undermine someone or a group in authority or an established order.

- **Insurrection** is a revolt against civil authority or an established government. Barabbas, the prisoner who was released instead of Jesus, was accused of leading an insurrection. (See Mark 15:7.)

- **Insubordination** is defiance of authority, disobedience to directives, misbehavior and misconduct. Stubbornness is also considered insubordination in I Samuel 15:23.

- **Usurp** means to take without right and make use of by force. Saul, the first king of Israel, usurped the priest's office by offering up sacrifice unto the Lord. (See 1 Samuel:13:8-14.) Absalom, through deceit, usurped the throne of his father, David, and made himself king. (See 2 Samuel 15:1-12.) Athaliah, daughter of Ahab and Jezebel, took the throne by force and made herself queen over Judah after killing her grandsons. (See 2 Kings 11:1-16.)

The aforementioned terms describe how a person responds when rebellion rules in his/her heart.

When a heart is filled with haughtiness, God despises it because it has become a place where witchcraft reigns.

Witchcraft goes against everything God is. It defies Him, because a person who operates in witchcraft uses a power other than God to achieve his/her goals. Servants of God must be subject to God and those He has appointed as authorities in earth.

One of the reasons God hates rebellion is that it gives birth to strife. Strife is aggressive conflict, dissension and discord. James 3:16 states that, *"For where envying and strife is, there is confusion and every evil work."* According to 1 Corinthians 3:3 and Galatians 5:20, strife is a work of the flesh. God lists strife among the seven deadly sins in Proverbs 6. *" . . . And he that soweth discord [strife] among the brethren" (v.19).*

Why was it important to spend some time on this topic, you may be asking? Because of the importance of our call — and the shift God is making in these last days in the earth through the dance — it is not surprising that the enemy will use whatever he can to thwart the plans of God; even if it means working through us. If we cannot be submissive to God and God's order, we cannot glorify Him in the dance or in any area of life and ministry. We cannot worship God with an impure heart. John 4:24, states, *"God is a Spirit: and they that worship Him must worship Him in spirit and in truth."* The psalmist declares, *"Who shall ascend unto the hill of the LORD? Or who shall stand in His holy place? He that hath clean hands, and a pure heart, who hath not lifted up his soul unto vanity, nor sworn deceitfully"* (Psalm 24:3-4).

Available for God's use.

As dance ministers, we must realize that we are not our own; we have been chosen to carry and reflect the glory of God. In doing so we abandon our will and aspiration and give ourselves completely to the will of God so that He may use us to usher in His presence. Making ourselves available to Him includes our body, our time, and our resources. If we were to step back and view things from a divine perspective, we would realize that who we are and what we own truly belongs to God. After all Romans 12:1 admonishes us to " *. . . present your bodies a living sacrifice, holy, and acceptable unto God which is your reasonable service.*" Because of the great things that God has done for us through the work of redemption, the least we can do is give ourselves wholly over to Him to be used according to His good pleasure.

Use resources to build and equip the ministry.
As we well know, the work of the ministry is not based solely on preaching and teaching the Word or even singing songs and dancing. It is also physically giving of our time, money, gifts, talents and skills to build and grow the ministry. In Exodus 25, God desired a sanctuary to dwell in, so He instructed Moses to have the people provide the resources to build Him a tabernacle. We know that God could have spoken into existence that which He desired as He did the universe, but He relied on the good will of the people to provide the resources instead. In doing so God gave them an opportunity to participate in the building of His sanctuary — and this was an act of worship. (See Exodus 25:1-8, 35:4-9, 20-29.)

We live in a fast-paced world and some of us have become caught up in the hustle and bustle of life. Nevertheless, what God requires has not changed. We are to be in the world but not of the world. God expects us to spend time serving in our ministry assignment. He still requires us to give as He as prospered us. Our giving allows us to participate in equipping and building the ministry.

Are you still excited about putting on your dancing shoes? I pray your answer is "yes!"

A Word for the Fifty-Something Plus

At this point, I would like to share a word that God spoke in my spirit while attending a dance conference. He said, "Ignite the fire in the 50 and over." God has called many people to the dance ministry who feel that their time has passed. They believe that since they did not answer the call or opportunities did not present themselves when they were younger, it is now too late. God says, "No!" He impressed in my spirit that once a call is upon our lives and a gift is given, it is forever. As a matter of fact, Romans 11:29 states, *"For the gifts and calling of God are without repentance."* The word *repentance* in this passage means irrevocable, not able to be changed or unalterable. God does not take back His gifts and calling and He is the only One who can give a command to stop using the gifts or to lay them down.

As a 50-plus person, God uses me in the dance to stir up the desire in older people. The worship arts are not reserved for the children, teenagers and 20-somethings. Usually, the older saints are more mature spiritually than the younger ones and, therefore, can minister more effectively in the spirit than the younger ones. A mature person has been through many struggles and tests in life. They have had many experiences with God, and they can draw out of the depth of their experiences. As a 50-something plus, you might not be able to kick up your legs, twirl or leap, but if you can move any part of your body, you can dance. Maybe you can minister with flags, streamers, banners, billows or other praise instruments. Personally, I minister with a flag as well as—if not better than—most young people.

There may be some men who fall in this category; however, I believe most of you are women. Women have been oppressed and told what they can and cannot do for so long, and many have embraced the lie. They have put themselves behind everyone else or simply have taken themselves off the list to become cheerleaders for others. God encourages us that it is the time to burst forth and use the gifts, talents and skills that He has placed inside of us.

It is never too late to answer God's call or to use His gifts. Many who are 50 and over, especially women, have returned to school and earned college degrees and started new careers. Older people, generally, are wiser, more reliable and take life more seriously than their younger counterparts. I was 40 when I returned to school to earn my graduate and post-graduate degrees. I was 50-something when I answered my call to the dance ministry. Not only am I dancing before the Lord, but also I am teaching others in the worship arts, have written a book on the subject and have established a worship institute. *In Pursuit of His Presence Worship Institute* (IPHPWorship.org) is sensitive to the needs of the 50-something plus and encourages them to allow the Lord to draw on the well of dance deposited in them. I did not have the knowledge, wisdom or skill to do this as a younger person. To everything there is a season, and might I add, everyone's season is different. Fifty-something women and men of God, it is your season! Step out with the boldness and confidence that if God has called you, He will sustain you.

Your Appearance Matters

According to an old English Proverb, "Clothes don't make the man." I agree with this statement. Jesus made this very clear when He was talking to the Pharisees regarding their legalistic ways. He taught that what is on the inside of a person is far more important than his/her outward appearance. Furthermore, Proverbs 31:30 tells us that, *"Favour is deceitful, and beauty is vain: but a woman that feareth the LORD, she shall be praised."* This verse implies that outward appearances are not as important as our fellowship with God. Even though clothes do not make the man or the woman, appearance does matter. First of all, people make judgments of who we are, what culture we are affiliated with, and what we can and cannot do based on our manner of dress. In the church we have embraced a newfound freedom in the way we dress. We are so careful not to appear legalistic that in some instances we have taken too much liberty. The Bible does command us, especially women, to dress in modest apparel. (See 1 Timothy 1:9.) God has never commanded us to do anything that is not for our good. The word "modest" in this passage means appropriate, decent and in good taste. Before I discuss what is and what is not appropriate for a dance minister while ministering before the Lord, I will deal with why we should present ourselves in appropriate apparel.

The congregation is usually a mixed group of people who are assembled for worship. Most people come to church to receive instructions, to be edified, to be healed, to be delivered, to find comfort and to find answers to their life situations. The dance minister, as I stated previously, has not only been called to minister to God, but to the needs of the people. Therefore, if he or she presents him/herself in an inappropriate manner, the likelihood exists that he/she will be more of a stumbling block than a minister of healing and deliverance. For example, some men are struggling with lust issues or normal natural desires. A dance minister who is inappropriately dressed is not going to minister to their spirit man. I have seen men drop their heads when some women are ministering in clothing that is too tight, sheer, low cut or too short. The congregation of saints should be a place that men can go and not have to struggle because of a female dance minister's inappropriate attire. It's like if you were to go to the hospital to receive treatment for an illness, but the doctor comes in and gives you medication that worsens the condition.

It is also important to realize that not only are there men struggling, but some also come to church to "enjoy the show." Yes, pedophiles attend the church, so let us not feed them bait. In addition, there is a spirit of homosexuality that has been released in the earth in greater measure. There are women in the church lusting after other women, and men lusting after other men. Can we keep it real? This should give you an idea of why we should dress appropriately when ministering in the dance. The most important reason for wearing appropriate attire is to glorify God. Remember, God takes pleasure in the dance. Do not abort your purpose for dancing by dressing immodestly.

What is inappropriate and appropriate dress?

- Garments that are ill-fitting, too tight or too short. The dance minister's body form should be covered. I know some would argue that God gave us these bodies and He wants us to put them on display. Yes, He did give us these beautiful bodies, however while we are ministering is not the time or place to reveal our shape.

- Garments that have low-cut necklines are inappropriate when an undergarment or overlay is not worn to build up the neckline. Am I saying that you need to wear your garments to cover your neck? No. For a good garment check, stand in the mirror, lean over and see if you can see any part of your breast or cleavage. If so, you need to cover that area with your garment or an overlay.

- Garments made of thin, sheer or see-through fabrics are only appropriate when worn with undergarments that cover the panty lines and bras. God has blessed some of us with a full-figure; therefore, we need to pay special attention to supporting our parts that move with us. Sport bras and firm fitting leggings should do the job.

- Garments worn with no undergarments are in appropriate. When we move as we dance, our dresses and skirts lift. Since they do, we need to wear leggings or tights and in many cases palazzo pants underneath the garment. You might be saying, "I don't lift my legs or twirl as I dance." Well, that might be true, but remember we are to be prepared to do whatever God desires to do through us as we minister in the dance. When palazzo pants are worn as the outer garment, leggings or tights should be worn underneath. Ideally, the top or overlay should be long enough to cover the buttocks area.

- Accessories that distract are inappropriate. Unless the accessories are a part of the garment or costume to help communicate the message, they should fade into the background. Oversized, flashy, dangly, colorful jewelry can be distracting. Remember, the goal is to minister and usher in the presence of the Lord for healing, restoration, deliverance, hope and encouragement. Ministering before the Lord is not a Broadway show.

- Men have a responsibility to dress appropriately as well. Unitards worn without overlays or long shirts, which show body form and private parts are ill-suited for ministry.

- Parents or guardians, please dress young children modestly as well, because pedophiles could be watching. Also, it sets a good example for them as they mature.

Some pastors have not embraced the idea of a dance ministry in their churches because they have been turned-off by those who did not present themselves properly. As you can see, the dance ministry and the dance minister are an integral part of worship. There is an anointing and heavy responsibility that a dance minister carries. It is not to be taken lightly, foolishly or unadvisedly. If God's commands are too stringent for you, maybe you should consider whether you are ready to submit to the authority of God and whether you have been called to minister before the Lord.

As dance ministers we are priests and our dance garments should be priestly. God gave Moses instructions on how the priests' garments were to be made. God also told Moses why they were to be made according to His pattern; "... *for glory and for beauty.*" (See Exodus 28.) God wanted to be glorified through the priests' garments and He wanted them to be beautiful. Our God is a God of beauty. He made His creation beautiful. Beautiful dance garments are pleasing to the eye and therapeutic; they can lift one's spirit and bring pleasure to God. The colors and embellishments of the garments all speak to God and communicate with the audience. When dance ministers are selecting garments for ministry, they should consider what message they are trying to convey to the audience. For example, if the message is salvation, red or silver or a combination of both should be worn. Red is the color of our Savior's blood. Without the shedding of blood there is no remission of sin. (See Hebrews 9:22.) We can glean from Scripture the symbolic meaning of many colors. The study of color symbolism tends to vary from source to source. However, over the years I have learned the meaning of some colors through personal study of the Scripture and biblical resources. You can find a list of some of the basic colors at the end of chapter 10.

It is preferable that we have artisans that God has anointed and appointed to create our worship garments rather than have them made in a factory or an assembly line by ungodly people. Artisans are workers in a skilled trade, especially ones that involve making things by hand. Remember, God selected and anointed artisans to work with Moses on the building of the tabernacle and He is still anointing and appointing artisans to create in the earth what He has in His heart in the heavens. God is restoring what has been lost or stolen from His people by the enemy and through our own ignorance. God has always intended for hands He has anointed to design and create His sacred instruments and garments. Let's examine Exodus 31:1-6:

> And the LORD spake unto Moses, saying, See, I have called by name Bezaleel the son of Uri, the son of Hur, of the tribe of Judah: And I have filled him with the spirit of God, in wisdom, and in understanding, and in knowledge, and in all manner of workmanship, To devise cunning works, to work in gold, and in silver, and in brass, And in cutting of stones, to set them, and in carving of timber, to work in all manner of workmanship. And I, behold, I have given with him Aholiab, the son of Ahisamach, of the tribe of Dan: and in the hearts of all that are wise hearted I have put wisdom, that they may make all that I have commanded thee;

God gave Moses the vision and instructions for making the tabernacle, but He did not intend for Moses to do it alone. He had already prepared skilled workers to come along side Moses and do various tasks. The Bible does not state this, but I believe that God gave Noah skilled help to build the ark.

Remember "The Law of First Mention?" This law simply means that whenever something or a subject matter is first mentioned in the Bible, the concept, principle or idea that it conveys remains throughout the Bible. The Godhead, the three in One, created the heavens and the earth. The work that God is doing is too big for one person.

Care of the Garment

The garments that we wear to minister before the Lord should be taken care of with the utmost care. They have been anointed and consecrated to the Lord's service and should be treated gently and respectfully as if God was wearing them Himself. If possible, separate your worship garments from your regular clothing. I know we do not always have the proper space, but it is preferable that they be hung in a separate place and laundered separately from the household clothing. This might seem extreme, but not so when we are giving honor to the King of kings.

What About Lifestyle?

We have settled the question of the call. We know that we should be people of character. We know that age is not a barrier and we know how to present ourselves. Now we need to discuss the lifestyle of the dance minister. However, first things first. Have you been born-again? We cannot assume that everyone who participates in church ministry has accepted Jesus Christ as their personal Savior. People are endowed with natural talents, skills and gifts and they can operate beautifully from any of these perspectives. However, to minister in the Spirit, we need to be born of the Spirit. We cannot glorify God if we do not belong to God. Only those who have made a confession of faith in Jesus Christ are His children.

The Spirit itself beareth witness with our spirit, that
we are the children of God . . .
—Romans 8:16

For ye are all the children of God by faith in Christ
Jesus.
—Galatians 3:26

That if thou shalt confess with thy mouth the Lord
Jesus, and shalt believe in thine heart that God hath
raised him from the dead, thou shalt be saved. For
with the heart man believeth unto righteousness; and
with the mouth confession is made unto salvation.
—Romans 10:9-10

Now lets take a few minutes and settle this issue. If you
have a desire to make a confession of faith in Jesus Christ,
pray this prayer aloud and from your heart.

Lord Jesus, I realize that I am a sinner and I need your
forgiveness. I believe that you died on the cross for
my sins, was buried and rose again from the grave.
I ask you to come into my heart, forgive me of my
sins and cleanse me from all unrighteousness. Lord,
I thank you for accepting me as your child. Amen!

If you prayed this prayer and believed in your heart,
you have been born-again. To put it another way, you are
SAVED. You must now grow in your new faith. Find a Bible
believing and teaching church that will assist you in your
growth in Christ.

Are You a Worshipper?

Dance as God created it, is for His pleasure. It is one of the elements of praise and worship. We have discussed praise, but what is worship? As most scholars will tell you, worship is better expressed than defined. However, I will list a few Hebrew and Greek terms that are used to describe or define worship. The word that is used most frequently in Hebrew is:

- **Shaha -** to bow down.

The first time this word appears in the Hebrew Bible is in Genesis 18:2 when Abraham was visited by the three men who brought the news that Sarah would bare a son, " . . . *and [he] bowed himself toward the ground.*" In 1 Samuel 15:25, "*shaha*" is used to mean coming before God in worship. "*Shaha*," translated as "worship," is mentioned the first time in Scripture in Genesis 22:5,

> And Abraham said . . . I and the lad will go yonder and worship, and come again to you.

The three more frequently used words in New Testament Greek for worship are:

- **Proskuneo** - to kiss toward, to make obeisance, do reverence to

This term was used by Jesus in Matthew 4:10,

> . . . Thou shalt worship the Lord thy God . . .

- **Sebomai** - a feeling of devotion, to revere

But in vain they do worship me, teaching for doc-
trines the commandments of men.

—Matthew 15:9

Saying, This fellow persuadeth men to worship God
contrary to the law.

—Acts 18:13

• **Latreuo** - to serve, to render religious service or
honor

For we are the circumcision, which worship God in
the spirit, and rejoice in Christ Jesus, and have no
confidence in the flesh.

—Philippians 3:3

These terms express worship from a biblical perspective.

The English word that we use today comes from an Old
English word "worthy-ship." It means to ascribe worth to.
When God is the object of our worship, we are ascribing
worth to Him.

My definition for worship is: entering into the presence
of God and enjoying His fellowship. Have you ever noticed
individuals in the congregation or in the choir dancing before
the Lord? Or have you seen persons leading in worship
enjoying what they are doing so much so that it seem that
they are caught up into another realm? They have entered
the realm of the Spirit and some respond with tears flowing
down their faces as their knees give way to a bow in adoration to the King of kings. This is an example of worship.

When we give ourselves over to God—whether in
singing, reading the Word, dancing, praying, working, caring
for our families, or driving on the freeway—we are ascribing
worth to God. He meets us where we are and fellowship
takes place. This is worship. Worship is a lifestyle. It is who

we are. We can worship anytime and anywhere. Jesus said, He is seeking true worshipers, those who will worship Him in spirit and in truth.

> But the hour cometh, and now is, when the true worshippers shall worship the Father in spirit and in truth: for the Father seeketh such to worship him. God is a Spirit: and they that worship him must worship him in spirit and in truth.
>
> —John 4:23-24

Worship flows from the heart. It is not some mindless activity that we do because we are prompted to do so. Once we have experienced the realm of the Spirit with God, we are not satisfied with anything less. Our spirit man will continue to yearn to meet with God. With Him nothing around us matters when we are in that place with God. There is joy in worship, peace, comfort, healing and deliverance. This is why the enemy hates to see us worshiping God; not only does he crave it for himself, but he also knows it is a safe place. It is a place where he cannot traffic and God is being exalted.

True worship is complete abandonment. During worship, worshipers forget about time, agendas and surroundings. They are lost and engulfed in the sweetness and glory of the Holy One. Worship is a humbling experience because flesh must die. According to 1 Corinthians 1:29, " . . . *no flesh should glory in his presence.*"

Many people cannot enter into this type of glory experience because their flesh hinders them. Pride stands at the door and cries, "You do not want to look stupid." "You do not want to seem weak." "You do not want to lose control." "What will others think of you?" "And besides, all of this is not necessary." That's why Jesus proclaimed, " . . . *If any man will come after me, let him deny himself, and take up his cross daily, and follow me*" (Luke 9:23). We must put our old man to death and be renewed in the spirit of our minds if we are going to give our all to the King of Glory. Again, I ask . . . "Are you a worshiper?"

The object of worship is to exalt the name of our Lord. On many occasions in the Word we are commanded to exalt His holy name. David, the king of Israel, was a worshiper and He exalted the name of the Lord and invites us to join in the celebration.

Give unto the LORD the glory due unto his name; worship the LORD in the beauty of holiness.

—Psalm 29:2

O magnify the LORD with me, and let us exalt his name together.

—Psalm 34:3

Make a joyful noise unto God, all ye lands: Sing forth the honour of his name: make his praise glorious.

—Psalm 66:1-2

Sing unto God, sing praises to his name: extol him that rideth upon the heavens by his name JAH, and rejoice before him.

—Psalm 68:4

Sing unto the LORD, bless his name; shew forth his salvation from day to day.

—Psalm 96:2

Enter into his gates with thanksgiving, and into his courts with praise: be thankful unto him, and bless his name.

—Psalm 100:4

Let them praise the name of the LORD: for his name alone is excellent; his glory is above the earth and heaven.

—Psalm 148:13

Let them praise his name in the dance: let them sing praises unto him with the timbrel and harp.

—Psalm 149:3

The name of the LORD is a strong tower: the righteous runneth into it, and is safe.

—Proverbs 18:10

And in that day shall ye say, Praise the LORD, call upon his name, declare his doings among the people, make mention that his name is exalted.

—Isaiah 12:4

By him therefore let us offer the sacrifice of praise to God continually, that is, the fruit of our lips giving thanks to his name.

—Hebrews 13:15

Those are just a few of the Scriptures that command us to lift up the name of our God. When we do, it is praise and worship. For those who desire to become a worshiper, but do not know how to start the journey of experiencing the presence of God, take a cue from David and begin to magnify the name of the Lord. The Lord our God is called by many names, titles and descriptions. Listed below are a few to get you going. Notice they are listed in alphabetical order to aid the memory. I am not suggesting that you learn these by rote. As you get comfortable lifting up the names of the Lord, they will begin to rise up out of your spirit.

Lord you are:

- Alpha and Omega
- The Almighty God (El Shaddai)
- Beginning and the Ending
- The Bread of Life
- The Branch
- The Creator of all things
- The Door
- The Divine One
- My Deliverer
- The Eternal God
- The Everlasting Faster
- First Fruit from the Dead
- My Faithful God
- The God of Grace
- The God of Abraham
- The Holy God
- My Hope
- My Healer (Jehovah Rapha)
- Immanuel
- The Great I AM
- Jesus
- A Jealous God
- The Judge
- Jesus Christ the Lord
- My Joy
- Kind God
- The Keeper of Israel
- The King of Glory
- The King of Kings
- The Lord of Lords
- The Lamb of God
- The Light of the World
- The Long-suffering God

- The Mediator between God and man
- The Merciful One
- The Most High God
- My Master
- The Bright and Morning Star
- The God who draws Near
- The Omnipotent One
- The Omnipresent God
- The Omniscience God
- The Only God
- My Precious, Powerful, Passover Lamb
- My Prince of Peace
- My Provider (Jehovah Jireh)
- Quick and Powerful
- The Righteous One
- My Redeemer
- The Rock of my salvation
- My Refuge
- My Savior
- The Shepherd of my soul
- The Sovereign God
- The All-Sufficient God
- The Son of God
- My Source
- My Strong Tower
- My Strength
- My Shelter in the time of storm
- The Triumphant One
- The True God
- The Truth, the Way and the Light
- The Understanding God
- The Vicarious God
- A Very Good God
- A Wise God, A God of Wisdom
- The Wonderful Counselor

- The Word of God
- An X-tra Special God
- A Zealous God

When we express to God who He is, it brings pleasure to Him and it makes us realize just how magnificent our God is. We begin to see Him with new eyes and in fresh ways. It brings peace and satisfaction to the soul. Remember, once you tap into His presence, there is no turning back. God will no longer have to long for you, you will say like the psalmist,

As the hart panteth after the water brooks, so panteth my soul after thee, O God. My soul thirsteth for God, for the living God: when shall I come and appear before God?

—Psalm 42:1-2

Are You Prepared to Minister?

Spiritual preparation is the most important aspect of ministering. God does not call us into ministry because we are prepared. The call alerts us to our assignment. However, we need to prepare ourselves for the assignment. Many people think because they are gifted and anointed, that they are prepared to launch out into ministering to God's people. God wants us to have character, integrity, compassion and love for His people. Operating skillfully in a gift does not mean we have character.

As you probably have heard before, a gift can take you places but only character can keep you there. After I accepted my call to preach God reminded me on many occasions, that *"A man's gift maketh room for him, and bringeth him before great men"* (Proverbs 18:16). In other words, God was telling me the gift He gave me would open doors for me and introduce me to great people. However, the one thing He never said nor implied was that I would be able to take advantage of the open door. If we are not prepared when the door opens—that is, if we have not allowed God to build character, integrity and endurance in us—the open door could be a curse instead of a blessing. All of us have seen many gifted people in ministry and other arenas of life climb the so-called ladder of success only to fall. They were just as gifted after they failed as they were before the fall. Now they have a gift, but no place to exercise it. People seem to remember our failures more than our successes. God wants our latter to be greater than the former. He moves us from faith to faith, strength to strength and glory to glory.

God does not want us to fail; therefore, He allows a period of preparation before elevation. When the call manifests, God is saying, "get ready, get ready, get ready." In other words, prepare yourself for the work. For some of us, it means getting some training or going to school. All of us need mentors and spiritual leaders who can impart wisdom, challenge us, correct us and attest to our preparedness.

God placed the bar high for those who minister before Him and His people. James 3:1 states in the NJKV, *"My brethren, let not many of you become teachers, knowing that we shall receive a stricter judgment."* God judges ministers stricter because we influence people. People can be misled by what we teach and by our example. That is why we need to live a life that models Christ. The apostle Paul lived an exemplary life, and he admonished his followers to follow him as he followed Christ. *"Be ye followers of me, even as I also am of Christ"* (1 Corinthians 11:1).

Dance ministers, we must have a devotional life; a life devoted to spending time with God. This is the only way we can grow spiritually and develop an intimate relationship with the Father, thus exemplifying Christ in our daily walk.

There is a story told in Luke 10:38-42, of two sisters, Martha and Mary. Jesus gave them a visit one day. Martha became distracted with preparing a meal while Mary sat at Jesus' feet.

> Now it came to pass, as they went, that he entered into a certain village: and a certain woman named Martha received him into her house. And she had a sister called Mary, which also sat at Jesus' feet, and heard his word. But Martha was cumbered about much serving, and came to him, and said, Lord, dost thou not care that my sister hath left me to serve alone? bid her therefore that she help me. And Jesus answered and said unto her, Martha, Martha, thou art careful and troubled about many things: But one thing is needful: and Mary hath chosen that good part, which shall not be taken away from her.

This story teaches us that we cannot allow the cares of this world to take priority over spending time with God. Jesus stated that Mary had chosen the good part. Mary had her priorities in order. Spending time worshiping God is more important than working for God. Many times we are anxious about working for God when we have not spent the proper time at His feet, which Jesus said was the best part.

If we have not spent time with God, we should not attempt to minister. Leaders who are praying for us will recognize when we are not spiritually prepared and should not allow us to minister. Lack of a devotional life leads to sin. This takes us back to the subject of submission. If we have submitted ourselves to spiritual authority we will submit and correct our actions. True worshipers spend time during the day and night enjoying God through song, praise, reading His word, praying, dancing, meditating or just sitting quietly in His presence. Dancing before the Lord does not need to be technically correct artistry, it just needs to flow from the heart of a worshiper to be effective. Again, I ask, are you a worshipper?

Since ministry affects those we are ministering to, we need to seek to live pure lives. Sin in our lives will have a negative affect on the atmosphere. Holding grudges, unforgiveness, hatred, strife, sexual sins and selfishness are just some examples of sin that hinders worship in the dance. Seek to live at peace with all men. Staying connected to the Vine (Jesus Christ) in true worship will give us power over sinful behavior.

The Importance of the Anointing

The word anointing has been overused and abused in Christendom. *Anoint* means to smear or rub with oil; to consecrate to an office of religious service. The anointing with oil in this case is symbolic of the Holy Spirit. A person or thing is consecrated or set apart for the Lord's service. The anointing is enabling power and symbolizes the work of the Holy Spirit in one's life. Without the Spirit anointing we cannot live God honoring lives. The following are examples in Scripture where anointing was applied.

Priest in the Old Testament were anointed.

And he poured of the anointing oil upon Aaron's head, and anointed him, to sanctify him.
—Leviticus 8:12

Kings and Prophets were also anointed when they were installed in their offices.

And the men of Judah came, and there they anointed David king over the house of Judah.
—2 Samuel 2:4a

And Jehu the son of Nimshi shalt thou anoint to be king over Israel: And Elisha the son of Shaphat of Abelmeholah shalt thou anoint to be prophet in thy room.

—1 Kings 19:16

Jesus was anointed.

The Spirit of the Lord is upon me, because he hath anointed me to preach the gospel to the poor; he hath sent me to heal the brokenhearted, to preach deliverance to the captives, and recovering of sight to the blind, to set at liberty them that are bruised, To preach the acceptable year of the Lord.

—Luke 4:18-19

Jesus spoke these words of prophecy that were first spoken by the prophet Isaiah. (See Isaiah 61:1.) Jesus was anointed or consecrated to do the work of ministry at His baptism. When He came up out of the water, the heavens opened and the Holy Spirit in the shape of a dove alighted upon Him.

Yes, Jesus functioned under the power of the anointing. He healed the sick, raised the dead, worked miracles, ministered the Word and drew the masses by the power of the anointing. When we are born-again, that is born of the Spirit, we are anointed to do the same works that Jesus did. Individually we are given gifts of service, which are anointed of God. There are varying degrees of the anointing on one's life depending on our assignment and our yielding to the Holy Spirit.

The anointing destroys yokes—severs bondage and afflictions—according to Isaiah 10:27:

And it shall come to pass in that day, that his burden shall be taken away from off thy shoulder, and his yoke from off thy neck, and the yoke shall be destroyed because of the anointing.

The anointing opens up the eyes of our understanding and gives us revelation of who God is and aids us in discerning between truth and error.

But the anointing which ye have received of him abideth in you, and ye need not that any man teach you: but as the same anointing teacheth you of all things, and is truth, and is no lie, and even as it hath taught you, ye shall abide in him.

— 1 John 2:27

Those, whom God has called to the ministry of the dance, are anointed of God to dance before Him and His people. It is the anointing that enables us to hear, see, move and express the love and heart of God. The anointing on the dancer's life invades the atmosphere, communicates a message from God and causes desired results. It could be healing, deliverance, comfort, hope, peace, joy, or simply to captivate the attention of the audience to usher them into the presence of the Lord. Without the anointing, the dance would just be beautiful artistry.

As we yield ourselves to God in obedience and spending intimate time with Him, we can increase the anointing on our lives.

Think On These Things

After reading *The Dance Minister*, I need to make the
following adjustments . . .

_____

_____

_____

_____

_____

_____

_____

_____

_____

_____

_____

_____

_____

_____

_____

_____

_____

_____

_____

_____

_____

_____

_____

_____

Chapter Eight

Me, A Servant?

"Dancing with the feet is one thing, but dancing with the heart is another."
—Anonymous

As a dance minister, have you ever considered yourself a servant? If not, I have great news for you. Because you have been called of God to minister before Him, you are His servant. The term "servant" in the Greek is *duolos* and is defined as a slave; one who receives instructions from his master and obeys without reservations. All born-again believers in Christ Jesus are His servants. The question is, are you a faithful servant? As was stated before, we live in a selfish era. Many want power and name recognition. However, the only power that we should desire is spiritual power and authority. This is done through the spirit of humility and ministry of serving. The life of Jesus clearly demonstrates this point.

Jesus came to earth declaring that He did not come to be served, but to serve and to give His life a ransom for many. (See Mark 10:45.) Jesus was given power and authority because He served faithfully and unselfishly according to Philippians 2:5-11:

> Let this mind be in you, which was also in Christ Jesus: Who, being in the form of God, thought it not robbery to be equal with God: But made himself of no reputation, and took upon him the form of a servant, and was made in the likeness of men: And being found in fashion as a man, he humbled himself, and became obedient unto death, even the death of the cross. Wherefore God also hath highly exalted him, and given him a name which is above every name: That at the name of Jesus every knee should bow, of things in heaven, and things in earth, and things under the earth; And that every tongue should confess that Jesus Christ is Lord, to the glory of God the Father.

Because Jesus humbled Himself as a servant, God gave Him a position of power and authority. What does this example teach us? " . . . *The servant is not greater than his lord; neither he that is sent greater than he that sent him*" (John 13:16). Jesus' mindset was totally different from those He came to serve and the world as we know it now. The world today encourages us to put ourselves at the top of the list and grab whatever we can get with as little effort as possible. Unfortunately, many come into the kingdom of God with this same mindset.

This selfish attitude is not new; Jesus witnessed it among those that He served. While Jesus was dining at the house of one of the chief rulers of the Pharisees, He taught a lesson on character and how to achieve greatness in His kingdom.

> When thou art bidden of any man to a wedding, sit not down in the highest room; lest a more honourable

man than thou be bidden of him; And he that bade thee and him come and say to thee, Give this man place; and thou begin with shame to take the lowest room. But when thou art bidden, go and sit down in the lowest room; that when he that bade thee cometh, he may say unto thee, Friend, go up higher: then shalt thou have worship in the presence of them that sit at meat with thee. For whosoever exalteth himself shall be abased; and he that humbleth himself shall be exalted.

—Luke 14:8-11

I am sure this must have astounded His listeners. It would seem unthinkable to give up a seat that would put them in the spotlight. How can anything powerful come out of this? The kingdom of God is an "upside down kingdom" in comparison to the world's kingdom. Jesus was dealing with the issue of pride. He explained to His listeners that it would be quite embarrassing to be presumptuous and take the best seat, then be asked to step down, to move lower. Rather, take the lowest seat, the seat of least importance; perhaps you might be invited to sit at the head table with the honoree. Then you will be honored indeed. We have too many people in the kingdom who want to sit at the head table. They want to be superstars. There is only one Superstar in the kingdom of God and His name is Jesus. He is the Star of David. The rest of us are just the "dust balls" of the earth who have been given light because of the servant attitude of Jesus, the Superstar.

Many occasions presented themselves for Jesus to teach on servanthood and greatness in His kingdom. A mother had the audacity to come right out and ask Jesus if her sons could have the highest seats in His kingdom:

Then came to him the mother of Zebedee's children with her sons, worshipping him, and desiring a certain thing of him. And he said unto her, What wilt thou? She saith unto him, Grant that these my two sons may sit, the one on thy right hand, and the other on the left, in thy kingdom. But Jesus answered and said, Ye know not what ye ask. Are ye able to drink of the cup that I shall drink of, and to be baptized with the baptism that I am baptized with? They say unto him, We are able. And he saith unto them, Ye shall drink indeed of my cup, and be baptized with the baptism that I am baptized with: but to sit on my right hand, and on my left, is not mine to give, but it shall be given to them for whom it is prepared of my Father. And when the ten heard it, they were moved with indignation against the two brethren. But Jesus called them unto him, and said, Ye know that the princes of the Gentiles exercise dominion over them, and they that are great exercise authority upon them. But it shall not be so among you: but whosoever will be great among you, let him be your minister; And whosoever will be chief among you, let him be your servant: Even as the Son of man came not to be ministered unto, but to minister, and to give his life a ransom for many.

—Matthew 20:20-28

I must say this mother had guts. But to think that her children were more deserving than anyone else is taking selfishness and pride to another level. Yes, I know all mothers want their children to achieve and do well in life, but to think your children are the ultimate . . . Wow! As much as Jesus loved the sons of Zebedee, James and John, He did not hold back His thoughts but made this opportunity a teachable moment. Jesus let this mother know, she did not truly understand what she was asking. His response to her was in the form of questions, however, the answers were embedded in the questions. Basically, Jesus was saying to her, are you ready for your sons to suffer what it takes to be awarded the best seats? Are you ready to drink the dregs, the garbage of sin that I am going to partake of? Jesus never said that we cannot be great, but there is a process to greatness. This process is achieved through walking in humility and having a servant's attitude.

The Process to Greatness

In the world's system you can achieve greatness—that is, power and fame by having a beautiful voice; inventing a product; offering a service; having the gift of gab; being wealthy and by committing a crime. Not so in God's kingdom. There is no place for self-aggrandizement. There is a process to greatness and it starts with humility, the place where it also began with Jesus. " . . . *He humbled himself, and became obedient unto death, even the death of the cross."* (Philippians 2:8b) We are admonished many times in the Word to humble ourselves if we want to be exalted. A few Scriptures are listed below.

Whosoever therefore shall humble himself as this little child, the same is greatest in the kingdom of heaven.
—Matthew 18:4

And whosoever shall exalt himself shall be abased; and he that shall humble himself shall be exalted.
—Matthew 23:12

But it shall not be so among you: but whosoever will be great among you, let him be your minister; And

whosoever will be chief among you, let him be your
servant: . . .

—Matthew 20:26-27

For whosoever exalteth himself shall be abased; and
he that humbleth himself shall be exalted.

—Luke 14:11

. . . For every one that exalteth himself shall be abased;
and he that humbleth himself shall be exalted.

—Luke 18:14

But ye shall not be so: but he that is greatest among
you, let him be as the younger; and he that is chief,
as he that doth serve. For whether is greater, he that
sitteth at meat, or he that serveth? Is not he that sitteth
at meat? But I am among you as he that serveth.

—Luke 22:26-27

Humble yourselves in the sight of the Lord, and he
shall lift you up.

—James 4:10

Humble yourselves therefore under the mighty hand
of God, that he may exalt you in due time: . . .

—1 Peter 5:6

The word *humble* is *tapeinoo* in the Greek and it means
to make low; bring oneself low. A humble person is one
without pride, arrogance or self-exaltation. He or she willingly submits to God.

Even though we have been admonished to humble ourselves, we usually do not obey this command without God
having to take us to a place of brokenness. However, our
flesh, the devil and the world war against us making the deci-

sion. God uses situations to foster humility. It is at this place where we evict pride, arrogance, haughtiness, rebellion, stubbornness, boasting and bragging. We also get rid of the I, me and my syndrome.

The process of brokenness can be a perplexing experience. Things begin to happen in our lives and we wonder or question what is going on. God is allowing the pressures of life to bring out the greatest in us. Before coal becomes a diamond, it withstands many years of darkness and pressure. It starts out dark, ugly and of little value. But after many years of enduring the pressure it becomes brilliant, crystallized and valuable—a diamond . . . a girl's best friend. There are no shortcuts to greatness. We are not going to start out today and become a wonder overnight. Jesus said, if you want to become great, become a servant, a slave, a *doulos*. As dance ministers, we have to settle the question, "Who is our master?" For Jesus said, *"No servant can serve two masters: for either he will hate the one, and love the other; or else he will hold to the one, and despise the other"* (Luke 16:13). If Jesus is our Master, then we must serve Him. Jesus did not call superstars, He called servants. This then means we have to develop the attitude that Jesus demonstrated throughout His life and ministry.

A servant, in the ancient world, did not sit at the table, they waited on tables. They did not seek to be seen. They had no rights, privileges, wants or desires; their wish was their master's command. Servanthood is not about position or power, however, it puts one in a position of power.

The reason that the apostles had powerful ministries is because they understood servanthood. In their epistles, they introduced themselves as slaves, bondservants of Jesus Christ.

Paul, a servant of Jesus Christ, called to be an apostle, separated unto the gospel of God, . . ."
—Romans 1:1

Paul and Timotheus, the servants of Jesus Christ, to
all the saints in Christ Jesus which are at Philippi,
with the bishops and deacons: . . .
                                        —Philippians 1:1

Paul, a servant of God, and an apostle of Jesus
Christ, according to the faith of God's elect, and the
acknowledging of the truth which is after godliness;
. . .
                                              —Titus 1:1

James, a servant of God and of the Lord Jesus Christ,
to the twelve tribes which are scattered abroad,
greeting.
                                            —James 1:1

Paul reminds us that we no longer belong to ourselves,
our bodies belong to God. "*What? Know ye not that your
body is the temple of the Holy Ghost which is in you, which
ye have of God, and ye are not your own? For ye are bought
with a price: therefore glorify God in your body, and in your
spirit, which are God's*" (1 Corinthians 6:19-20).

What God Requires of Servant Leaders?

Being a servant of the Lord Jesus Christ calls for radical
thinking and a lifestyle of obedience. It also requires a consecrated life to be a true servant of God.

Humility. This is the first quality that a servant must possess. It is the opposite of pride. Moses was called the most
humble man on the face of the earth during his day. (See
Numbers 12:3.)

Loyal. Faithful, devoted, trustworthy, committed, dedicated and dependable are all terms to describe loyalty. In what we call "back in the day," people were so trustworthy that written contracts were not necessary. People merely shook hands on a deal, and it was binding. During biblical times, confirmation on a deal, especially that of transfer of property, was done by taking off the shoe and giving it to another.

> Now this was the manner in former time in Israel concerning redeeming and concerning changing, for to confirm all things; a man plucked off his shoe, and gave it to his neighbour: and this was a testimony in Israel. Therefore the kinsman said unto Boaz, Buy it for thee. So he drew off his shoe.
>
> —Ruth 4:7-8

Well happy days are gone! Loyalty is a lost virtue in the 21st century. We write contracts and renege on them before the ink dries. Lawmakers make laws to protect people who make deals and then refuse to keep their end of the bargain. Chapters 7, 11, 12 and 13 bankruptcies are running rampant. Marriage vows are taken lightly, evident by the number of divorces per year. People hop from church to church with no regard for being planted in the house of the Lord. These are all signs of the perilous times that God said would come. Perilous times are times that are hard to deal with. God said during the last days,

> Men shall be lovers of their own selves, covetous, boasters, proud, blasphemers, disobedient to parents, unthankful, unholy, Without natural affection, truce-breakers, false accusers, incontinent, fierce, despisers of those that are good, Traitors, heady, highminded, lovers of pleasures more than lovers of God; Having

a form of godliness, but denying the power thereof: from such turn away.

—2 Timothy 3:2-5

Even though times have changed and have become more difficult, God's requirements of servanthood remain the same. *"Moreover it is required in stewards, that a man be found faithful"* (1 Corinthians 4:2). God rewards faithfulness. Ruth, the Moabitess, was found faithful and God rewarded her. She committed her life to serve an older bitter woman, Naomi, her mother-in-law. Ruth traveled 30 miles from her homeland to a place she had never seen. She was a Gentile who humbled herself and came under the advisement of her mother-in-law. She did not know the culture or how she would be received; yet she pledged to restore and bring back the gleam in a broken woman's life, who had no desire to be restored. Ruth's poem is often quoted, but how often is it practiced?

For whither thou goest, I will go; and where thou lodgest, I will lodge: thy people shall be my people, and thy God my God: Where thou diest, will I die, and there will I be buried: the LORD do so to me, and more also, if ought but death part thee and me.

—Ruth 1:16-17

Because of her loyalty, Ruth's name is mentioned in the genealogy of Jesus Christ. (See Matthew 1:5.) I am sure Ruth never dreamed that she would be so honored. However, God's word is true, " . . . [s]he that humbleth [her]self shall be exalted" (Luke 14:11b).

Another good example of a loyal servant is Elisha. He was a faithful servant of Elijah.

So he departed thence, and found Elisha the son of Shaphat, who was plowing with twelve yoke of oxen before him, and he with the twelfth: and Elijah passed by him, and cast his mantle upon him. And he left the oxen, and ran after Elijah, and said, let me, I pray thee, kiss my father and my mother, and then I will follow thee. And he said unto him, go back again: for what have I done to thee? And he returned back from him, and took a yoke of oxen, and slew them, and boiled their flesh with the instruments of the oxen, and gave unto the people, and they did eat. Then he arose, and went after Elijah, and ministered unto him.

—1 Kings 19:19-21

Once Elijah threw his mantle on him, symbolizing that Elisha was being given the authority to operate in the prophetic office and would eventually succeed Elijah, Elisha started putting things in place to serve Elijah. Elisha, a wealthy man, stopped in the middle of plowing the fields and started preparing a farewell party to celebrate his new assignment. He used his plowing equipment as firewood to cook the meal. Elisha was serious about his call. There was no chance of him returning to his former career. He made a definitive decision and did not look back. After the celebration, he followed Elijah and poured water on his hands. (See 2 Kings 3:11.) Elisha was not too wealthy or anointed to do menial tasks.

Because of Elisha's faithful service to Elijah, he was rewarded with a double portion of Elijah's anointing and worked twice the miracles of Elijah. (See 2 Kings 2:9-10.)

Courage. Servants are to be courageous. Courage means strength to persevere in the face of danger and extreme difficulty. Proverbs 24:10 declares, *"If thou faint in the day*

139

of adversity, thy strength is small." While serving in the kingdom of God we will face many adversities and oppositions. We must have boldness to overcome every hurdle. We will not achieve much for God if we are cowards. Servanthood is not for shrinking violets or the faint-at-heart.

When Joshua was commissioned to succeed Moses, God commanded that he be of good courage, to be very courageous. The way to become courageous is to know your God. The more experiences we have with God, the more we trust Him, and consequently, we become bolder and stronger in our faith. For this reason God commanded Joshua to stay in the Word, meditate on the Word day and night. (See Joshua 1:8.) As we read and mediate on God's promises and what He has done in the past, we are encouraged and convinced that we can do everything He has ordained us to do, because we know that He is with us. Furthermore, 1 Corinthians 10:11 states, *"Now all these things happened unto them for ensamples: and they are written for our admonition, . . ."* God has given us written history of His faithfulness to past generations. He has also declared that He is immutable, that is, He does not change. (See Numbers 23:19; James 1:17; Hebrews 13:8.) Moreover, He assures us that He is not a respecter of persons, which means He is impartial. (See Acts 10:34.) If He did it for one generation, He will do it for the next.

Deborah, the only female judge mentioned in Scripture, was a woman of great courage. (See Judges 4, 5.) She served during Israel's dark and turbulent days. During the days of the judges, there was no king in Israel and everyone did what they thought was right in their own eyes. It was a time of chaos, self-will and degradation. Because of Israel's state of wickedness, God allowed other nations to oppress them. Before Deborah's rule, they had been oppressed for 20 years by the Canaanites. The Canaanite army was very powerful and Israel's army paled considering the multitude that Sisera, the leader of the Canaanite army, had at his disposal, not to mention Sisera's nine hundred iron chariots. The Children of Israel cried out to God in their usual fashion and God raised up Deborah to lead them. In spite of her seemingly disadvantaged position, Deborah faced the opposing army with courage, knowing God would make good on His word to deliver Sisera into her hand. (See Judges 4:7.) The Lord was with Deborah and Barak, the captain of Israel's army, therefore, they defeated their enemy. (See Judges 4:14-15, 23-24.) Israel enjoyed rest for 40 years because of Deborah's courage.

Unlike, Joshua and Deborah, we have the Holy Spirit living on the inside of us, the ever abiding presence of God. There is no reason for us not to rise to the occasion and face opposition fearlessly. After all, God has declared that we are more than conquerors.

> Nay, in all these things we are more than conquerors through him that loved us. For I am persuaded, that neither death, nor life, nor angels, nor principalities, nor powers, nor things present, nor things to come, Nor height, nor depth, nor any other creature, shall be able to separate us from the love of God, which is in Christ Jesus our Lord.
> —Romans 8:37-39

Cost. There is a cost to being a servant. Servant leadership is costly because it is a sacrifice.

Mary, the mother of Jesus, paid a high price when she humbled herself and allowed God to use her womb as the incubator for His Son. She was a young unmarried woman. She could have been stoned to death for being pregnant out of wedlock, according to the Levitical laws. Her engagement to be married was put in jeopardy. Joseph had planned to put her away privately. Yet, Mary, upon hearing that she was chosen to bring the Son of God into the world, and who considered herself to be a maidservant of the Lord, unreservedly, announced to God, "*. . . Be it unto me according to thy Word*" (Luke 1:38b). In other words, no price was too high for Mary to pay. She was God's servant and whatever God wanted to do through her, she was willing to do.

Many of us receive beautiful cards at Christmas time depicting the birth of our Savior on that blessed night. But, have you ever considered what Mary had to endure? She accepted the word of the Lord but there was a cost. Mary endured nine months of baby blues: bloating, backaches, morning sickness, cravings, swollen feet and weight gain, just to name a few. The picture does not get any better on her delivery day either. She had to bring her precious child into the world on a hard cold floor in a stall reeking with animal feces filled with pesky flies.

Dance ministers, we are menservants and maidservants of God. God does not ask us to do anything that will not cost us something. If it does not cost anything, it is not worth offering to God. David, the king of Israel, lived by this principle. In 2 Samuel 24:24b, David said, "*. . . neither will I offer burnt offerings unto the LORD my God of that which doth cost me nothing.*"

Being a servant leader is a privilege and with that privilege comes some level of responsibility and obligation, which should not be considered a burden. As dance ministers, we need special garments and accessories in which to minister. I realize that everyone cannot spend top dollar for a garment; however, our garments should be fit for the King. In order to have nice garments, we might need to sacrifice a few others things, such as a closet full of shoes or a drawer full of gadgets. The costlier garments usually look nicer and have longer use. Our garments should be appropriate for the message that is being communicated. Therefore, we need a wardrobe of "priestly" garments. Praise instruments such as glory hoops, flags, banners, steamers and props also cost. Remember, anything we present to God should cost us something.

We must also sacrifice our time. We must spend time before the Lord seeking His face in prayer, reading and meditating on His Word. This should be done outside of the times we spend with Him to get a choreographed movement. We must exercise and keep our bodies in shape, this takes time. Also, it takes time to practice individually or with the group and to attend meetings. There are talents and skills that God has given us, other than the dance, that are needed in dance ministry such as: record keeping, teaching, and general duties. And, of course it takes time to minister before the Lord. Hopefully you will have noticed that the aforementioned responsibility and obligation amount to cost . . . the cost of being a servant leader.

The greatest cost is giving of ourselves. *"I beseech you therefore, brethren, by the mercies of God, that ye present your bodies a living sacrifice, holy, acceptable unto God, which is your reasonable service"* (Romans 12:1). Even though offering our bodies to God to use in His service is considered a cost, in the grander scheme of things, it is not. Jesus purchased us by dying on the cross for our sins. The cost associated for us is the willingness to submit to God in ministry instead of giving into the desires of the flesh. We allow God to use what He has already paid for. Paul reminds us of this in 1 Corinthians 6:19-20.

> What? Know ye not that your body is the temple of the Holy Ghost which is in you, which ye have of God, and ye are not your own? For ye *are bought with a price*: therefore glorify God in your body, and in your spirit, which are God's.
>
> —Emphasis added

As Paul stated in Romans 12:1, the least we could do for God after all He has done for us is to offer our bodies back to Him for His service. Remember, Jesus did not think is was robbery, even though He was God, to offer up His body on the cross, that we might have life and have it more abundantly. (See Philippians 2:6; John 10:10b.)

Risk-takers. Servants are risk takers. We sometimes run the risk of others taking advantage of us both in ministry and our personal lives. To some we may look foolish, and others may gossip about us behind our back. What compounds this even further is that even though we are sacrificing ourselves, we may feel unappreciated and unrewarded.

I am sure Noah looked foolish and was jeered for building a huge boat (the Ark) in the presence of a generation that had not seen rain before. Yet, he humbled himself and hammered away at the ark for 120 years as God promised there would be flood waters that would overcome the earth. Noah had the testimony that he pleased God. (See Genesis 6:3, 8-9, 17.)

Queen Esther, wife of Ahasuerus, King of the Medes and Persians, risked all by obeying the voice of the Lord. She served her people by saving them from sudden annihilation. Esther risked her life by entering the king's court without first being summoned by the King. This was an act punishable by death. In spite of what could have happened to Esther, she put the life of others before herself. God graced Esther with favor because she realized that she had been born and groomed for this purpose. (See Esther 4:13-16.)

Paul took risk on many occasions, traveling from city to city preaching the gospel to heathens. He speaks of many of the dangers that he faced in 2 Corinthians 11:23-28,

Are they ministers of Christ? (I speak as a fool) I am more; in labours more abundant, in stripes above measure, in prisons more frequent, in deaths oft. Of the Jews five times received I forty stripes save one. Thrice was I beaten with rods, once was I stoned, thrice I suffered shipwreck, a night and a day I have been in the deep; In journeyings often, in perils of waters, in perils of robbers, in perils by mine own countrymen, in perils by the heathen, in perils in the city, in perils in the wilderness, in perils in the sea, in perils among false brethren;In weariness and painfulness, in watchings often, in hunger and thirst, in fastings often, in cold and nakedness. Beside those things that are without, that which cometh upon me daily, the care of all the churches.

Jesus is our perfect model of a servant. He took the risk of being called a lying prophet, an impostor and a heretic; being betrayed by Judas, rejected by Peter and forsaken by the disciples. Knowing that all these things would take place, He remained focused on His mission, accepted the risks and left a perfect model for us to follow as servants.

Now before the feast of the passover, when Jesus knew that his hour was come that he should depart out of this world unto the Father, having loved his own which were in the world, he loved them unto the end. And supper being ended, the devil having now put into the heart of Judas Iscariot, Simon's son, to betray him; Jesus knowing that the Father had given all things into his hands, and that he was come from God, and went to God; He riseth from supper, and laid aside his garments; and took a towel, and girded himself. After that he poureth water into a bason, and began to wash the disciples' feet, and to wipe them with the towel wherewith he was girded. Then cometh he to Simon Peter: and Peter saith unto him, Lord, dost thou wash my feet? Jesus answered and said unto him, What I do thou knowest not now; but thou shalt know hereafter. Peter saith unto him, Thou shalt never wash my feet. Jesus answered him, if I wash thee not, thou hast no part with me. Simon Peter saith unto him, Lord, not my feet only, but also my hands and my head. Jesus saith to him, He that is washed needeth not save to wash his feet, but is clean every whit: and ye are clean, but not all. For he knew who should betray him; therefore said he, Ye are not all clean. So after he had washed their feet, and had taken his garments, and was set down again, he said unto them, Know ye what I have done to you? Ye call me Master and Lord: and ye say well; for so I am. If I then, your Lord and Master, have washed your feet; ye also ought to wash one another's feet. For I have given you an example, that ye should do as I have done to you. Verily, verily, I say unto you, the servant is not greater than his lord; neither he that is sent greater than he that sent him. If ye know these things, happy are ye if ye do them.

—John 13:1-17

Jesus could take the risk because He knew who He was. He did not have self-esteem issues. According to the above passage, He knew:

- God put all things in His power
- God was in control of His life and ministry
- He was the Son of God
- He came from God
- God was the source of His mission on earth
- He was confident that He was working the plan of God for His life
- He was returning to God
- He was returning to His eternal home as God

146

Jesus was confident in who He was and His mission here on earth. When we lack confidence, it is very difficult to take the risk of serving others. Jesus took off His outer garments and picked up the towel of servanthood because He was a risk-taker, modeling for His followers an act of true servitude. The disciples' feet were dirty from walking the dusty roads in Jerusalem. It was customary, in that day, for the host to provide a basin of water for guests to wash their feet. In this case, Jesus was the host; He arranged the dinner party. Jesus discerned the need and humbled Himself by kneeling and washing the disciples' feet.

This was a true act of humility, but more so, Jesus was teaching a lesson of servanthood—how we should serve one another in the kingdom of God. When He said in verse 15, *"For I have given you an example, that ye should do as I have done to you,"* He was not saying I want you to wash each other's feet. Rather, He was saying, I want you to serve one another. Do as I have done! I saw a need; I satisfied and fulfilled the need. That was Jesus' whole mission and His reason for coming to earth. He came as a Servant of His Father because they saw a need; A need for the sin debt to be cancelled. Jesus pleased His Father by paying the sin debt at the cross. *"Verily, verily, I say unto you, the servant is not greater than his lord; neither he that is sent greater than he that sent him. If ye know these things, happy are ye if ye do them"* (vv. 16-17).

If we want to be fulfilled and powerful, we need to do as Jesus did. Take the risk and serve as a minister of the dance ministering healing, deliverance, comfort, encouragement, joy and peace to everyone in your circle of influence. When we lead as servants with a spirit of humility by bringing ourselves low; that is when God will raise us up to heights unknown.

Serving is the Key to Advancement in Leadership

Many aspire to be in a position of authority. We are all leaders in the kingdom; however, the amount of authority that we will have depends on our loyalty of service. In Matthew 25:21, Jesus said to His servant, *"well done, thou good and faithful servant: thou hast been faithful over a few things, I will make thee ruler over many things. . ."* We have to be proven faithful to the task with which God has entrusted us, before He will elevate us. He starts us small then gives us more, as we prove faithful over the little. Many do not like to start small or at the bottom rung. They want to start at the same place with others who have been serving faithfully for many years. God knows that they do not have the strength of character to bear up under the weight, so He does not give it to them. In Zechariah 4:10, the question is asked, *"For who hath despised the day of small things?"* We are not to resent the little God has assigned to us, rather groom and nurture it so God can prosper it.

The following are great men and women in the Bible who served others and were proven faithful before God exalted them.

- Abraham served God by leaving his family and homeland before God entrusted him with great wealth and the promised child, Isaac. (See Genesis 12, 13, 18, 21.)

- Sarah served her husband Abraham and called him lord, before she was entrusted to carry the promised child, Isaac. (See Genesis 17; Hebrews 11:11.)

- Moses cared for his father-in-law Jethro's flock before he was called to lead the children of Israel. (See Exodus 3:1.)

- Joshua served as Moses' attendant before he became his successor. (See Exodus 24:13; Joshua 1:1.)

- Ruth served Naomi before she was entrusted with becoming the wife of a wealthy man, Boaz, who became the progenitor of the lineage of Jesus. (See Ruth 2, 4:13-22.)

- Elisha served Elijah by pouring water on his hands, became his apprentice and was later given a double portion of His anointing. (See 2 Kings 2:9, 3:11.)

- David served as a shepherd over his father's sheep on the backside of the mountain before becoming King over God's chosen people. He also served as Saul's armor bearer and musician to expel evil spirits. (See 1 Samuel 16:21.)

- The 12 Disciples served Jesus before they were commissioned as His successors. (See Matthew 10:1-4; Mark 3:13-19.)

- Timothy served under the tutelage of Paul before he was appointed an Elder in the church. (See 1 Timothy 1:2.)

"Moreover it is required in stewards, that a man be found faithful" (1 Corinthians 4:2). Who are you faithfully serving? According to Psalm 75:6-7, *"For promotion cometh neither from the east, nor from the west, nor from the south. But God is the judge: he putteth down one, and setteth up another.* God knows when we have been faithful in our post. When He is ready, He will do the promoting. No one can hinder or abort God's plan for our lives.

Yes, we are servants! And as servants we should maintain the standard and model that Jesus and others, in Scripture have set for us. Humility, obedience and commitment should be the pillars on which our ministry of service stands. In doing so, we will help to create an environment that fosters harmony with God and with one another.

Think on these Things

After reading *Me, A Servant?*, I realize I need to make
some attitude adjustments . . .

_____

_____

_____

_____

_____

_____

_____

_____

_____

_____

_____

_____

_____

_____

_____

_____

_____

_____

_____

_____

_____

_____

_____

Chapter Nine

The Power of Unity

"Dancing is moving to the music without stepping on anyone's toes, pretty much the same as life"
— Robert Brault

Were you ever asked to work on a group project in school? Each person in the group was responsible for a certain aspect of the project. In order for the project to be completed, each person had to perform his or her task. If one person in the group failed to complete his part, each person in the group received a less than perfect grade. The purpose of these types of assignments is to prepare the student for the real world. Working cooperatively with others is tantamount to completing tasks successfully. As humans, we need the help and support of others to survive.

Our basic human nature is self-centeredness. Therefore, we have to be taught to rightly relate to one another; in other words, learn how to give and receive. As a former kindergarten teacher, one of my responsibilities was to teach young children to share and to get along with one another. This was a daunting task, as the children had to make major adjustments in their thinking and behavior.

A famous line from *Meditation XVII*, written by an English poet, John Donne, says, *"No man is an island."* I understand Donne was a Christian preacher; therefore, I believe he might have formed his opinion from the verse found in the book of Romans, which states, *"For none of us liveth to himself, and no man dieth to himself"* (14:7). Donne, essentially was saying, human beings cannot live in isolation because all human lives are woven together. The Bible declares that people who isolate themselves are self-centered and unwise. (See Proverbs 18:1.) In other words, it is foolish to try to live alone with a mind-set that no one else matters. It takes the united effort of everyone to make this world a livable place.

One of the chief ways to get a heavenly response from God is to live in harmony with those of the household of faith. God calls it a good and pleasant thing. It brings glory to Him, to the point that He pronounces us blessed and gives us eternal life. (See Psalm 133.)

What is Unity?

The *New Oxford American Dictionary* defines unity as, harmony or agreement between people or groups, the state of forming a complete and pleasing whole; the quality or state of being made one.

From this definition we can glean some synonyms for unity: harmony, peace, agreement, wholeness, oneness, one accord, singleness, consensus and homogeneous. These are all terms that bring delight to God's heart. Some of these terms will be used in our discussion of unity. A good example of unity is found in the book of Genesis chapter 11.

And the whole earth was of one language, and of one speech. And it came to pass, as they journeyed from the east, that they found a plain in the land of Shinar;

154

and they dwelt there. And they said one to another, Go to, let us make brick, and burn them throughly. And they had brick for stone, and slime had they for morter. And They said, Go to, let us build us a city and a tower, whose top may reach unto heaven; and let us make us a name, lest we be scattered abroad upon the face of the whole earth. And the LORD came down to see the city and the tower, which the children of men builded. And the LORD said, Behold, *the people is one, and they have all one language;* and this they begin to do: and now nothing will be restrained from them, which they have imagined to do. Go to, let us go down, and there confound their language, that they may not understand one another's speech. So the LORD scattered them abroad from thence upon the face of all the earth: and they left off to build the city. Therefore is the name of it called Babel; because the LORD did there confound the language of all the earth: and from thence did the LORD scatter them abroad upon the face of all the earth (1-9, emphasis added).

Even though an evil work was being done, the people were faithfully working together to accomplish a common goal. They decided that they were going to build a tower to reach heaven and make a great name for themselves. God, Himself, recognized that the people were ONE; they were united in mind, purpose and effort. God even stated that because the people were united in purpose, nothing would stop them from reaching their goals. God seemed to imply that anything that they could dream up, they could achieve.

The people had ONE language—all of them spoke the same thing. They understood and agreed with each other and there was no strife or division among them. This sounds very good and commendable, except their plans were evil.

Isn't this just like human nature? People who do not like one another will unite their efforts to fight a common enemy or reach a common goal. Since the tower builders' deeds were evil, God confused their language. They might have been speaking the same words, but their minds could not translate or interpret what was being said. As a result, they had to stop building and go their separate ways.

The power of unity can also be seen in the book of 2 Chronicles after Solomon finished building the temple of God and was moving the Ark of the Covenant into the temple. The trumpeters and singers were in harmony as they lifted praise to God on cymbals, stringed instruments and harps.

> It came even to pass, as the trumpeters and singers were as one, to make one sound to be heard in praising and thanking the LORD; and when they lifted up their voice with the trumpets and cymbals and instruments of musick, and praised the LORD, saying, For he is good; for his mercy endureth for ever: that then the house was filled with a cloud, even the house of the LORD; So that the priests could not stand to minister by reason of the cloud: for the glory of the LORD had filled the house of God.
> —2 Chronicles 5:13-14

Positive illustrations of unity can be found in the book of Acts. God was able to do great and mighty things in the earth because the people were on one accord. For example, the Holy Spirit descended while 120 believers were united in prayer.

> And when the day of Pentecost was fully come, they were all with *one accord* in one place. And suddenly there came a sound from heaven as of a rushing

mighty wind, and it filled all the house where they were sitting. And there appeared unto them cloven tongues like as of fire, and it sat upon each of them. And they were all filled with the Holy Ghost, and began to speak with other tongues, as the Spirit gave them utterance.

—Acts 2:1-4, emphasis added

One of the most powerful historic events—the coming of the Holy Spirit to the earth—changed the course of the world and the church because the people stood as one.

God also worked many signs, wonders and miracles through the hands of the Apostles because the people were in harmony.

And by the hands of the apostles were many signs and wonders wrought among the people; (and they were all with *one accord* in Solomon's porch. And of the rest durst no man join himself to them: but the people magnified them. And believers were the more added to the Lord, multitudes both of men and women.) Insomuch that they brought forth the sick into the streets, and laid them on beds and couches, that at the least the shadow of Peter passing by might overshadow some of them. There came also a multitude out of the cities round about unto Jerusalem, bringing sick folks, and them which were vexed with unclean spirits: and they were healed every one

—Acts 5:12-16, emphasis added

The people received healing, deliverance and salvation, and the church grew due to unity. We can see how powerful unity is through these illustrations. No wonder the enemy works so hard to keep us self-centered and divisive.

God Hates Strife

As we discussed in chapter 7, strife is an abomination unto God. It is listed among the seven deadly sins in Proverbs chapter 6. (See Proverbs 6:16-19.) Strife is the opposite of unity. Some words to describe strife are: discord, disharmony, dissension, division, contention, envy, conflict, friction and hostility. All of these things God despises.

God hates this kind of behavior because it goes against who He is, His character, His person. He is Jehovah-Shalom, the God of Peace. He is the God of harmony, agreement, oneness and unity; and He will not commune in the midst of strife and discord. He asked, *"Can two walk together, except they be agreed"* (Amos 3:3)? Another reason God hates strife is because it thwarts or frustrates His plans for the world. Jesus said in His high priestly prayer, that the only way that the world will know that God sent Him into the world was by believers being one as He and the Father are one. (See John 17:20-22.) Paul dealt with the issue of discord on several occasions in his epistles to the churches. In the epistle to the Romans, he wrote:

> Be of the *same mind one toward another*. Mind not high things, but condescend to men of low estate. Be not wise in your own conceits.
> —Romans 12:16, emphasis added

> Let us therefore follow after the things which *make for peace*, and things wherewith one may edify another.
> —Romans 14:19, emphasis added

> Now the God of patience and consolation grant you to be *likeminded one toward another* according to Christ Jesus: That ye may with *one mind and one*

mouth glorify God, even the Father of our Lord Jesus Christ.

—Romans 15:5-6, emphasis mine

In these Scriptures, Paul is exhorting believers to actively and consciously do whatever it takes to live, serve and worship God in a spirit of harmony. In both of his epistles to the church of Corinth, he reminds the saints to be of the same mind.

Now I beseech you, brethren, by the name of our Lord Jesus Christ, that ye all speak the same thing, and that there be no divisions among you; but that ye be perfectly *joined together in the same mind and in the same judgment.* For it hath been declared unto me of you, my brethren, by them which are of the house of Chloe, that there are contentions among you. Now this I say, that every one of you saith, I am of Paul; and I of Apollos; and I of Cephas; and I of Christ. Is Christ divided? Was Paul crucified for you? Or were ye baptized in the name of Paul?

—1 Corinthians 1:10-13, emphasis added

Paul had heard that there was strife among the saints who met at the house of Chloe. He reminded them that there should be no division among them.

Finally, brethren, farewell. Be perfect, be of good comfort, *be of one mind, live in peace*; and the God of love and peace shall be with you.

—2 Corinthians 13:11, emphasis added

Paul could not end this second epistle to the church of Corinth without reemphasizing the importance of living in unity. He ended his statement with a promise that the God who is love and peace will abide with you. If we want our heavenly Father to abide with us, we must seek to live in harmony as members of the body of Christ.

While in prison awaiting trial, Paul's mind was on the welfare of the churches. He wrote several epistles to the churches. One of them was the letter of Ephesians that was an encyclical letter, a correspondence that was to be circulated among the churches in Asia Minor. Paul exhorted them to be united in the Spirit by earnestly seeking to live in peace.

> Endeavouring to keep the unity of the Spirit in the bond of peace.
>
> —Ephesians 4:3

The word *endeavouring* is *spoudazo* in the Greek, and it means to use speed, make effort, be diligent, labor, study, be prompt or earnest.[1] Unity does not just happen; we must labor to attain it. Why? Because, again, we are self-centered by nature, and we desire to have what we want when we want it, regardless of the desires or needs of others. This type of behavior should only be excusable for babes or toddlers at times.

The epistle to the Philippians was also one of Paul's prison epistles. He wrote this letter to the church at Philippi partly to address the subject of strife. While in prison, Paul heard that there was some dissension in the congregation. In each of the four chapters of this small letter, Paul addressed the subject of unity. In chapter one he pleaded with the church at Philippi to conduct themselves in a unified manner that exemplified Christ for the sake of the gospel.

> Only let your conversation be as it becometh the gospel of Christ: that whether I come and see you, or else be absent, I may hear of your affairs, that

ye stand fast *in one spirit, with one mind* striving
together for the faith of the gospel;
—Philippians 1:27, emphasis added

In Philippians 2:1-8, Paul throws some punches in the
Spirit. He seems a little fed up with the conduct of the saints
at Philippi. Listen to his discourse:

If there be therefore any consolation in Christ, if any
comfort of love, if any fellowship of the Spirit, if any
bowels and mercies, Fulfil ye my joy, that ye be *like-
minded,* having the same love, *being of one accord,
of one mind.* Let nothing be done through strife or
vainglory; but in lowliness of mind let each esteem
other better than themselves. Look not every man on
his own things, but every man also on the things of
others. *Let this mind be in you, which was also in
Christ Jesus*: Who, being in the form of God, thought
it not robbery to be equal with God: But made himself of no reputation, and took upon him the form
of a servant, and was made in the likeness of men:
And being found in fashion as a man, he humbled
himself, and became obedient unto death, even the
death of the cross.
—Emphasis added

Paul was basically saying if there were anything that the
saints could do to make his stay in prison more joyful would
be to hear that they are united in heart, mind and purpose.
He also hoped that everything that they were doing was for
the glory of God and not for self-exaltation. Most of all, Paul
was asking them to empty themselves the way Christ did and
lift up their fellow brothers and sisters in Christ.

Again in chapter three, Paul appeals to the saints to be
like-minded in the Spirit, especially the ones who are mature.

> Nevertheless, whereto we have already attained, let
> us walk by the same rule, *let us mind the same thing.*
> —Philippians 3:16, emphasis added

Finally, in chapter four Paul mentions two women in the church by name who were in conflict, Euodia and Syntyche. He urged them to reconcile.

> Therefore, my brethren dearly beloved and longed
> for, my joy and crown, so stand fast in the Lord,
> my dearly beloved. I beseech Euodias, and beseech
> Syntyche, that they *be of the same mind in the Lord.*
> —Philippians 4:1-2, emphasis, added

Paul had such a passion for these two women to reconcile that he asked one of the church leaders to help them. It is believed by some that these women were deaconess in the church.

As we have gleaned from the statements and exhortations from Paul, we recognize that he was very serious and adamant about believers being of the same mind and on one accord. Paul knew the power of unity and the consequences of strife and division; therefore, he was steadfast and uncompromising when it came to the subject of unity.

Peter also had a passion for unity. In 1 Peter chapters 2-3, after giving a discourse on submission, Peter urged everyone to, "*. . . be ye all of one mind, having compassion one of another, love as brethren, be pitiful, be courteous* (1 Peter 3:8).

Abraham, A Man Who Knew the Consequences of Strife

Abraham was known as a man of obedience and peace. When strife arose between his herdsmen and his nephew,

Lot, he immediately "put the axe to the root." Basically he quickly put an end to the strife because he did not want to be a party to conflict.

> And Lot also, which went with Abram, had flocks, and herds, and tents. And the land was not able to bear them, that they might dwell together: for their substance was great, so that they could not dwell together. And there was a *strife* between the herdmen of Abram's cattle and the herdmen of Lot's cattle: and the Canaanite and the Perizzite dwelled then in the land. And Abram said unto Lot, Let there be *no strife*, I pray thee, between me and thee, and between my herdmen and thy herdmen; for we be brethren. Is not the whole land before thee? Separate thyself, I pray thee, from me: if thou wilt take the left hand, then I will go to the right; or if thou depart to the right hand, then I will go to the left.
> —Genesis 13:5-9, emphasis added

Abraham was the older and wiser of the two and he knew that God would not continue to bless them in the midst of strife. Therefore, he took the initiative and devised a plan to settle the dispute. God is not the originator of, nor does He dwell in, contention as Paul stated in 1 Corinthians 14:33, *"For God is not the author of confusion, but of peace, as in all churches of the saints."*

Sometimes we have to separate ourselves for the sake of peace. According to Proverbs 22:10, if you, *"Cast out the scorner, and contention shall go out; yea, strife and reproach shall cease."* Abraham made the honorable choice and decided not to strive with his relative. God is still honoring his choice today, as his descendants are still being blessed for God is with them.

Unity in the Dance Ministry Is Not An Option

As we have ascertained from the aforementioned commands and exhortations, God abhors discord among believers. He especially hates it among worship ministers. This point is well illustrated in the penalty imposed on Lucifer, the first worship leader, when he caused dissension among a significant number of the heavenly praise and worship angelic hosts. God released him from his assignment and kicked him and all who followed him in the rebellion out of heaven never to enjoy His presence again. This should give us a very good idea of how strongly God hates disunity among His ministers of worship.

As we said before, the ministry of dance is designed to glorify God and restore order in the earth. How can strife discord and divisiveness, which is disorder, restore order? Chaos can only breed more chaos. God's purpose cannot be achieved through strife!

As dance ministers, some of us may be part of a team or group of dance ministers. Everybody cannot have their way or do their own thing. Someone must lead and the rest submit to leadership. Not only should there be harmony among the dancers, but the dance ministers must work in conjunction with other worship artists, such as the praise and worship leader, the choir, the banner and flag ministry, and the mime and step ministry. Furthermore, all the ministries must be in tune with the Pastor's vision and request. When all the ministries are on one accord, God is glorified, the people of God are edified, and as a result, the world will come to know Christ.

Satan, who was once Lucifer, is a mastermind of confusion. He will use anything and anybody to create disharmony among God's people, especially His worship artists. He hates God and he hates that God is using the "dust balls" of the earth to do what he was created to do—that is, bring Him pleasure through the worship arts.

The Source of Disunity

Satan, the enemy of our souls, is certainly chief among the reasons for a lack of unity, however the apostle James asks a question,

From whence come wars and fightings among you? Come they not hence, even of your lusts that war in your members?
—James 4:1

According to James, disagreements accompanied by infighting come from our own lust. The word lust in this passage (Greek *hedone*) means *pleasure or passion*. It is our own flesh that seeks to be pleasured that causes us not to live in harmony with our sisters and brothers. Due to our own lack of self-worth, our disappointments, and the hurts and pains we have experienced in life, we have perceptions that are distorted and we prejudge situations according to our own desire not to be hurt, disappointed or rejected again. This gives place to envy, jealousy and quarrels. James also states that,

For where envying and strife is, there is confusion and every evil work.
—James 3:16

The apostle Paul was disappointed with the church at Corinth because after preaching and teaching them the Word of God, they were still childish, which was evident by their envy, strife and divisiveness.

And I, brethren, could not speak unto you as unto
spiritual, but as unto carnal, even as unto babes in
Christ. I have fed you with milk, and not with meat:
for hitherto ye were not able to bear it, neither yet
now are ye able. For ye are yet carnal: for whereas
there is among you envying, and strife, and divisions,
are ye not carnal, and walk as men?
                                      — 1 Corinthians 3:1-3

As you can see, our own flesh and selfish ways are a
major source of disunity among believers. The teachings of
the world are also contrary to the will of God. The world
teaches the selfish message of looking out for number one —
self. However, the Word of God warns us not to attach ourselves to the world, and all of its lust, which is temporal and
is passing away.

Love not the world, neither the things that are in the
world. If any man love the world, the love of the
Father is not in him. For all that is in the world, the
lust of the flesh, and the lust of the eyes, and the pride
of life, is not of the Father, but is of the world. And
the world passeth away, and the lust thereof: but he
that doeth the will of God abideth for ever.
                                      — 1 John 2:15-17

How Can Unity Be Achieved?

If we are going to walk in the oneness of the Spirit, we
must first take off the old man, and be renewed in the spirit
of our minds.

That ye put off concerning the former conversation
[behavior] the old man, which is corrupt according
to the deceitful lusts; And *be renewed* in the spirit

of your mind; And that ye put on the new man, which after God is created in righteousness and true holiness.

—Ephesians 22-24, emphasis added

We must guard our hearts against offense. We must also have a desire to change and to please our heavenly Father. God will transform our behavior when we take the initiative and give Him permission.

We must walk according to the Word:

Walk in the Spirit—"This I say then, Walk in the Spirit, and ye shall not fulfil the lust of the flesh. For the flesh lusteth against the Spirit, and the Spirit against the flesh: and these are contrary the one to the other: so that ye cannot do the things that ye would." (Galatians 5:16-17)

Walk in humility—"Submitting yourselves one to another in the fear of God" (Ephesians 5:21). "Let nothing be done through strife or vainglory; but in lowliness of mind let each esteem other better than themselves." (Philippians 2:3)

Walk in Forgiveness and Love— "Put on therefore, as the elect of God, holy and beloved, bowels of mercies, kindness, humbleness of mind, meekness, long-suffering; Forbearing one another, and *forgiving one another,* if any man have a quarrel against any: even as Christ forgave you, so also do ye. And above all these things *put on charity [love],* which is the bond of perfectness. And let the peace of God rule in your hearts, to the which also ye are called in one body; and be ye thankful." (Colossians 3:12-15)

Walk in Covenant—when we partake of the Lord's table we are renewing the covenant we made with God and our fellow believers. Walk in that covenant. Don't merely go through the motion. Renew that commitment on a regular basis. (See 1 Corinthians 11:23-26.)

Walk in Peace—". . . seek peace, and ensue it" (1 Peter 3:11b).

Remember, no man is an island. Believers are one body in Christ Jesus. The Apostle Paul put it best when he said, *"There is one body, and one Spirit, even as ye are called in one hope of your calling; One Lord, one faith, one baptism . . ."* (Ephesians 4:4-5). Remember, we are servants, not superstars. It is not about us; rather, it is about doing the will of the Father.

Think On These Things

After reading *The Power of Unity*, I have a better understanding of . . .

_____

_____

_____

_____

_____

_____

_____

_____

_____

_____

_____

_____

_____

_____

_____

_____

_____

_____

_____

_____

_____

_____

_____

_____

Chapter Ten

Instruments of Praise, Worship and Warfare

"Never give a sword to a man who can't dance."
—Confucius

This book has been primarily about dance as a form of praise and worship. Many times, instruments or tools of worship accompany dance to help clarify what God is doing through His vessel or in the atmosphere. The following is a list of commonly used instruments:

Banners

Banners captured my attention in 1997 when I was drawn by their beauty and use in a worship service I attended. I tried to obtain information on the how's and why's of banners, but had no immediate success. In 2000, I heard an announcement on the radio about a local church sponsoring a banner-making workshop. I attended along with my daughter and another member of the church. We were taught the purpose of banners and how to make banners. I am a very creative and artistic person, so I jumped right in, and with the help of my daughter and the member who accompanied us, made our first banners—"Jesus" and "King of All the Earth." I was hooked! Since that time, numerous banners have been made and purchased by the church.

What is a banner?

According to *Webster's New World Dictionary-Third College Edition*, a banner is a piece of cloth bearing a design, motto, slogan, etc., sometimes attached to a staff and used as a battle standard.[1] *Strong's Exhaustive Concordance* defines banner: to flaunt, such as a to raise a flag; used figuratively to mean to be conspicuous (easy to see or perceive; obvious).[2]

The term banner or banners is used six times in the Authorized King James Version of the Bible. The term standard or standards, which is also translated as banner, is used 20 times in the KJV. Other terms that denotes banner is ensign, signals, sign and pole.

Banners serve many purposes. Listed are a few gleaned from Scripture:

- Banners Acknowledge the Presence of the Lord

    Then came Amalek, and fought with Israel in Rephidim. And Moses said unto Joshua, Choose us out men, and go out, fight with Amalek: to morrow I will stand on the top of the hill with the rod of God in mine hand. So Joshua did as Moses had said to him, and fought with Amalek: and Moses, Aaron, and Hur went up to the top of the hill. And it came to pass, when Moses held up his hand, that Israel prevailed: and when he let down his hand, Amalek prevailed. But Moses' hands were heavy; and they took a stone, and put it under him, and he sat thereon; and Aaron and Hur stayed up his hands, the one on the one side, and the other on the other side; and his hands were steady until the going down of the sun. And Joshua discomfited Amalek and his people with the edge of the sword. And the LORD said unto Moses, Write this for a memorial in a book, and rehearse it in the ears of Joshua: for I will utterly put out the remembrance of Amalek from under heaven. And Moses built an altar, and called the name of it Jehovah-nissi: For he said, Because the LORD hath sworn that the LORD will have war with Amalek from generation to generation (Exodus 17:8-16).

When Moses built the altar and named it Jehovah-Nissi, "The Lord is Our *Banner*," he was acknowledging that God was in the midst of them. He realized that it was neither his raised arms nor the rod that won the battle, but God. Banners are an indication that God is in the midst of us. Indeed, Jesus is our Banner as He was raised upon a pole (the Cross), and His body represented the redemptive power of God to free us from sin and to give us liberty.

- **Banners Display God's Truth and Cause the Enemy to Flee**

  Thou hast given a *banner* to them that fear thee, that it may be displayed because of the truth. Selah. (Psalm 60:4; emphasis added)

God is truth. When His name or His Word is displayed on a banner, His truth is established in the midst. The enemy cannot prevail where the truth of God is present. So the enemy is defeated by the display of banners.

Then shall the Assyrian fall with the sword, not of a mighty man; and the sword, not of a mean man, shall devour him: but he shall flee from the sword, and his young men shall be discomfited. And he shall pass over to his strong hold for fear, and his princes shall be afraid of the *ensign*, saith the LORD, whose fire is in Zion, and his furnace in Jerusalem (Isaiah 31:8-9).

- ### Banners Identify and Distinguish the Tribes

Every man of the children of Israel shall pitch by his own *standard*, with the *ensign* of their father's house: far off about the tabernacle of the congregation shall they pitch (Numbers 2:2; emphasis added).

God is a God of order. While the children of Israel were traveling through the wilderness, they did not camp just anywhere. God had a designated place for them to pitch their tents. Each tribe displayed a banner to identify their individual family camp.

- ### Banners Declare Victories

We will rejoice in thy salvation, and in the name of our God we will set up our *banners*: the LORD fulfill all thy petitions. (Psalm 20:5, emphasis added)

Banners are used to brag on or boast in the Lord. The children of Israel displayed banners to declare their God as the victor and to brag on the power that is in His name.

Thou art beautiful, O my love, as Tirzah, comely as Jerusalem, terrible as an army with *banners* (Song of Solomon 6:4; emphasis added).

Who is she that looketh forth as the morning, fair as the moon, clear as the sun, and terrible as an army with *banners* (Song of Solomon 6:10; emphasis added)?

The word "terrible" in these passages means "awe-inspiring or frightful." In other words an army with banners is striking, beautiful and peaceful to the victorious nation; however it is a frightful sight to the enemy.

- Banners Put the Enemy to Flight

So shall they fear the name of the LORD from the west, and his glory from the rising of the sun. When the enemy shall come in like a flood, the Spirit of the LORD shall lift up a *standard* against him (Isaiah 59:19; emphasis added).

Fear is struck in the heart of the enemy when God raises His banner; subsequently, he flees. The enemy knows he is no match for the great and terrible God.

- Banners Honor Our God

". . . And in the name of our God we will set up our banners: . . . " (Psalm 20:5)

Banners proclaim the worth of our God. They herald (display the good news of) His glory, honor and majesty.

- ## Banners Serve as a Focal Point for Healing

> And the LORD said unto Moses, Make thee a fiery serpent, and set it upon a pole: and it shall come to pass, that every one that is bitten, when he looketh upon it, shall live (Numbers 21:8).

> And as Moses lifted up the serpent in the wilderness, even so must the Son of man be lifted up: . . . (John 3:14).

Just as Moses erected the pole with the bronze serpent in the wilderness and those who looked upon it was healed; healing is still being released through the ministry of banners. Why? Because Jesus is the ultimate healer.

Banners release the anointing of God in the atmosphere. They are used as instruments of praise and worship, and as a symbol of God's presence, power and majesty. They can be displayed on stands, hung on a wall or used in processionals. They are made in various sizes and shapes, depending on how and where they are to be used. Larger banners can be seen and read from a distance. Banners made of attractive and lustrous fabrics, trims and embellishments are pleasing to the eye because they have a regal appearance. They also represent the glory and majesty of our King. Beautiful banners usually stir the emotions and can be cathartic. They are powerful praise and worship instruments that produce healing and deliverance.

Banners should be treated with special care and stored properly when not in use. Banner bearers should know the purpose of and how to carry and display banners.

Flags

The English word "flag" means a piece of cloth attached to a pole; but it is not found in the Authorized King James Version of the Bible. However, the term banner and flag can be used interchangeably, as flags serve the same purpose as banners. They identify, distinguish, rally; declare victory; puts the enemy to flight; and honors God. Flags are used to open the heavens and release the presence and power of God in the atmosphere. Many flags bear the names and symbols of God. They can be displayed on a stand, hung on a wall, used in a processional, twirled or waved.

Nations use flags as an emblem. They are symbols that reference the country. The flag of the United States is a welcoming relief to an American serving or lost in a foreign land.

Flags should also be cared for properly. Remember they are emblems of the Most High God.

Glory Hoops and Glory Rings

Glory hoops are usually circular in shape and resemble a tambourine with long streamers. They are used as a wave offering unto the Lord. Glory rings are rings with long streamers attached and they are worn on the finger. Glory hoops and Glory rings can be used to enhance the message the dancer is communicating or alone as a praise and worship instrument.

Tabrets or Tambourines

Tabrets, also known as tambourines and timbrels, are ancient instruments. They have been around since God created the heavenly beings. In Ezekiel 28, God gives a description of how He created Lucifer.

Thou hast been in Eden the garden of God; every precious stone was thy covering, the sardius, topaz, and the diamond, the beryl, the onyx, and the jasper, the sapphire, the emerald, and the carbuncle, and gold: the workmanship of thy *tabrets* and of thy pipes was prepared in thee in the day that thou wast created (Ezekiel 28:13; emphasis added).

Lucifer, now known as satan, was created with built-in tabrets. A tabret or timbrel is a small hand-held percussion instrument that resembles a drum. The first time tabrets/timbrels are mentioned in Scripture is in Genesis 31:27 when Laban reprimand Jacob for leaving him secretly.

Wherefore didst thou flee away secretly, and steal away from me; and didst not tell me, that I might have sent thee away with mirth, and with songs, with *tabret*, and with harp (emphasis added)?

The second mention of tabrets/timbrels is found in Exodus 15:20 after the children of Israel crossed the Red Sea.

And Miriam the prophetess, the sister of Aaron, took a *timbrel* in her hand; and all the women went out after her with *timbrels* and with dances.

Tabrets and timbrels are mention nineteen times in Scripture and are associated with dancing and merry making. They are beautiful instruments of praise and worship when used by anointed and skilled dancers or individual worshippers.

Billows

Billows are powerful praise and worship instruments. The term is used twice in the Authorized King James Version of the Bible.

Deep calleth unto deep at the noise of thy water-spouts: all thy waves and thy *billows* are gone over me (Psalm 42:7; emphasis added).

The Hebrew word that the psalmist uses for billows means something rolled, such as a "heap" of stone; a wave, a spring. The motion of the billow is like a rolling wave. As the wave rolls over us, our spirit calls out for the deep things of God and we can sense the presence of God. It is at the deep places that God does His greatest work in us. He cleanses and washes us and delivers us from those things that are not of Him.

For thou hadst cast me into the deep, in the midst of the seas; and the floods compassed me about: all thy *billows* and thy waves passed over me. (Jonah 2:3; emphasis mine)

Jonah used the Hebrew word *mishbar*, which has been translated as billows, and it means a breaker and wave.[3] Its primitive root means to burst, break and bring to birth. As the billows rolled over Jonah, he had a breakthrough. His will was broken and subsequently, he decided to obey the voice of the Lord.

The ministry of the billow breaks up the hard, crusty places in our lives and makes way for the Holy Spirit to birth the dreams and visions that God has placed in our hearts. When a woman is about to give birth, her water breaks first. As the billow rolls over us our water breaks and we bring forth that which God has deposited in us.

Billows can be used as a part of the worship service or anytime there is a need for a breakthrough.

Streamers

Streamers are long narrow strips of material usually attached to a dowel. They float in the wind and are symbolic of the presence of God. Streamers are used to invite the Holy Spirit into the atmosphere. They sometimes bear the names and symbols of the Lord.

Shofars

The word translated as trumpet in the Authorized King James Version of the Bible is the Hebrew word *showphar*. A shofar is a curved ram's horn used in biblical times by the children of Israel to make a sound. God commanded that they blow the shofar for various reasons; among them, to assembly the people and as a call to worship. The first time the shofar was used to make a sound can be found in the nineteenth chapter of Exodus.

> There shall not an hand touch it, but he shall surely be stoned, or shot through; whether it be beast or man, it shall not live: when the *trumpet* soundeth long, they shall come up to the mount (Exodus 19:13; emphasis added).

> And it came to pass on the third day in the morning, that there were thunders and lightnings, and a thick cloud upon the mount, and the voice of the *trumpet* exceeding loud; so that all the people that was in the camp trembled (Exodus 19:16; emphasis added).

And when the voice of the *trumpet* sounded long, and waxed louder and louder, Moses spake, and God answered him by a voice (Exodus 19:19; emphasis added).

God, Himself, blew the shofar to gather His people at Mt. Sinai. Likewise, a trumpet will sound as a signal of Christ's return to gather the saints.

In a moment, in the twinkling of an eye, at the last trump: for the trumpet shall sound, and the dead shall be raised incorruptible, and we shall be changed. (1 Corinthians 15:52)

The shofar was an integral part of Jewish life in biblical days and the tradition continues today. Many churches today are using the shofar as a part of their worship experience.

Crowns

A crown is an ornament worn on the head as a symbol of honor and royalty. A Greek word for crown is *stephanos*. Kings and queens wear a *stephanos* as an emblem of majesty and supremacy. When we minister with the crown, we are giving honor and glory to the King of Kings. It says the King is present and in charge. The psalmist asked, "Who is the King of glory?"

Lift up your heads, O ye gates; and be ye lift up, ye everlasting doors; and the King of glory shall come in. Who is this King of glory? The LORD strong and mighty, the LORD mighty in battle. Lift up your heads, O ye gates; even lift them up, ye everlasting doors; and the King of glory shall come in. Who is this King of glory? The LORD of hosts, he is the King of glory. Selah (Psalm 24:7-10).

The religious people mocked Jesus and placed a crown of thorns on His head during His crucifixion; however, He will be wearing a golden crown when He returns to reap His end-time harvest.

And I looked, and behold a white cloud, and upon the cloud one sat like unto the Son of man, having on his head a golden *crown*, and in his hand a sharp sickle (Revelation 14:14; emphasis added).

Jesus Christ is King of all the earth.

These praise and worship instruments are commonly used in the ministry of dance and in the praise and worship service. They add splendor and meaning to what we wish to convey to God and minister to those in attendance. They are also tools used by the worshipper to usher in the presence of the Lord and change the atmosphere. The worship instruments are created in a variety of colors to represent the multifaceted dimensions of our God.

Color Symbolism

Color	Meaning
Red	Life (color of Christ's blood); Redemption
Blue	Heavenly Authority
White	Purity; Holiness, Undefiled

Color	Meaning
Gold	Divinity
Bronze	Repentance
Silver	Redemption
Green	Life; Refresh; Prosperity, Growth
Purple	Royalty, Majesty
Black	Humility; Mourning, Evil
Brown	Humanity
Pink	Passion, Joy

Think On These Things

After reading *Instruments of Praise, Worship and Warfare*,
I have a better understanding of . . .

_____

_____

_____

_____

_____

_____

_____

_____

_____

_____

_____

_____

_____

_____

_____

_____

_____

_____

_____

_____

_____

Epilogue

I pray this book has been a blessing to you and your ministry. It has been my joy to share the Word of the Lord with you. As I mentioned in chapter one, God called me to the ministry of the dance as a mature person. One of the ways that He uses me is to stir up the gift of dance in the 50 and over. Not only do I minister in the dance, but God also used me to establish a worship institute, *In Pursuit of His Presence Worship Institute* (IPHP). His mandate to me was to lay a foundation in the worship arts ministry. He said, "Many are dancing, but they do not know why they are dancing." Even though the Institute has a strong emphasis on dance, it also surveys all aspects of worship. Our mission is to provide biblically-based education and mentorship to a generation of individuals who desire to consistently pursue the presence of God through dance and as a lifestyle.

The goals and objectives of the Institute are:

- To create an atmosphere where the Spirit of God finds habitation;
- To ignite the desire to minister in the dance; to provide knowledge on the purpose of the dance;
- To share biblical knowledge on how to live in the power of the Holy Spirit;

- To develop a heart of servant-hood through the art of leadership;
- To introduce creative and prophetic choreography, and the usage of praise instruments;
- To be a source of mentorship and encouragement for ministers of the dance;
- To be one of the greatest dance institutes that exemplifies the glory of God and the intent of the kingdom as it relates to the dance ministry.

Some of the topics discussed concern: the purpose of the dance, proper restoration of the dance, you as a worshipper, what God expects of the dance minister and more.

The Institute provides a nine-month program, where the students meet for class and training once a week. Both the students and the faculty are blessed beyond measure by what God is doing through us. We are looking forward to expanding the Institute to monthly regional seminars. For more information and to view the full program of study, visit our Web site (IPHPWorship.org).

What the Students are Saying:

This class is a blessing! I've been blessed to learn so much more about the heart of a worshipper, and the significance of being called to minister in dance to effectively reach people. I cherish the relationships I've been able to establish with the women here. The instructors are well versed, knowledgeable, and genuinely caring. I'm telling all my friends about IPHP! Be blessed and be a blessing. (Nadine Mahoney)

This school is an answer to my prayer for a deeper knowledge of God's purpose and desire for dance in the church. I'm only a third of the way through the course, but I feel like I'm being equipped spiritually and mentally to never be made to second guess this form of worship. I'm learning that everything that's powerful in pulling down strongholds, satan stole from God's people. But praise be to God for raising up schools like IPHP to fill us with revelation knowledge of the power of worship, to bring order anywhere there is chaos. *Abba-Father, continue to bless the instructors with an abundance of wisdom, peace, boldness, strength and grace to continue to build your army of worshippers, in the mighty name of Jesus!!!* (Tarsha Washington)

Every Monday I wake up with expectancy, joy and anticipation at the fact that this is my day to attend the IPHP Worship Institute. When I first signed up I thought I was going to a dance class, but this is so much more. It's a meeting place where God dwells. Every Monday He meets in this wonderful place and speaks to me through these anointed Women of God! I am honored and privileged at being taught by Apostle Caretha Crawford, Minister Hewlette Pearson, Master Teacher Ruth Franks and Elder Pamela Sorrells. Through them I have learned more about being in the presence of the Most High God, what it means to be a bearer of His presence, and to know that I am chosen and a royal priesthood; and that before time I was predestined to be a part of this awesome teaching! I tell everyone who will listen about the blessing of being a part of this ministry and encourage all to come and join us as we continue to be In Pursuit of His Presence! (Jeronn Russell.)

WOW! IPHP is truly a blessing. I look forward to going to class every Monday and I get filled with the information that ALL the teachers are providing.

They are very loving and caring women of God. They teach with passion and fire, and I enjoy every bit of it. This class is awesome because it's not just about dancing; it's about learning the foundation as to why you worship in dance. In order to do something to the fullest, you must understand why you do what you do, and that is what these wonderful women are providing through IPHP. I have longed for a class such as this and God opened the door for me. I found out about the class literally three hours before the first class started. I showed up that night and have never stopped going. My friend told several people about the class, and she said, however, I was the only one who showed. I know this is where God wanted me to be and I am blessed to be on the receiving end of such awesome teaching. I liked it so much I brought my mom with me, and she enjoys it and looks forward to attending every week as well. If you want to attend this class, do not hesitate, I didn't and I'm glad. Be blessed. (Audrey Jones)

In Pursuit of His Presence has ignited my fire to seek God all the more, and get into His presence, and to live a righteous life. As a student I have been blessed more and abundantly than what I could ever hope for. Wow! What a blessing to be in the presence of powerful, humble and anointed women of God. Their preparation and labor before the Lord are evident in every session. I drive into class every Monday night as my Spirit leaps for joy with the anticipation of entering into His presence. (Cilily Brown)

Being a professional student, I have studied many many subjects and believe in getting multiple certificates for everything I undertake. In the past, I have taken a class to learn the art of liturgical dance in the church. I am so glad to have found IPHP Worship Institute. This school has exceeded my expectations in gaining valuable knowledge about how dance is related to worship, God, and the church. The information is presented in a very logical manner, which lends itself to learning the fundamental basics for this style of worship arts. The instructors are very knowledgeable and easy to learn from. The atmosphere is pleasant and makes learning there enjoyable, and I look forward to attending classes each week. May God's favor rest upon this institute. I highly recommend attending this institute for learning the dance as a part of the worship arts. (Dr. Venetta Kalu)

I praise God for bringing IPHP into my life! I know that I am in the right place to learn and glean from such beautiful women of God (our instructors) the biblical principles of dance and why we dance. In addition to that, we are also learning about *Worship: The Heartbeat of God*, where we examine ourselves to know whether we are worshippers of the Most High. What an experience it has been thus far! It has been a blessing to learn these and many more lessons under these real women of God. They have a passion for God and His presence that is contagious; when we all come together we experience His Presence and draw from the well of knowledge God has given us through our instructors who have clearly been Holy Spirit led throughout our classes. I look forward to learning more and more self-examination as I sit and learn the things God has ordained through this (His) Institute for me! You will experience God here and be blessed by the biblical teachings as it relates to how we shall glorify Him with the dance through the worship arts! (Joy Jordan)

Praise be to God. Thank you Apostle for opening up IPHP Institute. IPHP is the answer to my prayer. Not only have I learned what it means to be a true worshipper and servant, I have learned in this short time how to truly get into the presence of God. IPHP has been a blessing in my personal life as well. (C. Odom)

Let me just say... I have been blessed! I would like to personally thank Apostle Crawford for the vision of "IPHP." These instructors and Women of God have shared knowledge in such an informative way that I can never repay them on any monetary level. They have blessed this first class and I know they will forever continue God's work. Did you know God created dance for us to worship Him...and for so much more? We start our Monday nights out worshipping in the presence of God through song. Our lessons and teachings are supported biblically, so you must have your Bible (the Sword). But before we have time to get in a good "Amen...Hallelujah or just a Thank you, Father," the Holy Ghost kicks in and it's on....the presence of the Lord...it's here! So if you are seeking a place where you can learn how to be a true worshipper through the arts, give IPHP a call. Apostle Crawford, and the ministerial staff (Hewlette Pearson, Pamela Sorrells and Ruth) are all filled with a loving spirit that just keeps you coming back week after week. I have faith that this atmosphere is quite pleasing to our Father in heaven. Continuous blessings, I pray. (Monquie C. Brown, Founding Student Class 2011)

WOWWWWWWW. IPHP has blessed me in many ways. I am just so excited for what the Lord has been doing through me as I am getting into His Word more. God just keeps blessing me and my daughter over and over. God blessed me with a new job and my daughter is healed and healthy!! God is still dealing with me on the inside. I've been broken before Him two times already and saw Him manifest in me. IPHP has really opened my heart to receive all the things God wants me to have. I thank God for IPHP and what it is doing right now and for the future He has in store. The devil is nagging, but God has given me the strength to not look back, but to keep moving forward for what He has in store for me. Amen. God bless!! (Candace Burrell)

I want to begin by saying "TO GOD BE THE GLORY." I was seeking a training like this and guess what? God opened up the door and I am enrolled at IPHP. I did not realize how awesome these training classes were, but "God is an awesome God!" My session on Monday can actually take me to Sunday. IPHP has been a tremendous blessing to my spirit, body and soul. And learning to dance to the words first and then add the music is very powerful. I thought dancing for the LORD was just like in the world where you just get up and do it. By coming to IPHP, I have learned that dancing for the LORD comes from your spirit, heart and soul. You minister to hurting souls and to unbelievers to be saved. I'm encouraging many people to come and be blessed at IPHP. If you don't dance you will do something when you leave. I'm taught by four great women of God (Apostle Crawford, Minister Pearson, Master Teacher Ruth Franks and Elder Sorrells) and this is an honor. I want you to know "I am a gift from God to the Kingdom and the nations of the world; and I have positive qualities that are coming to light in my personal life and ministry every day." All to God's glory. (Margaret L. Ford)

I enjoy the classes at IPHP. It is apparent that Apostle Crawford has much experience and she knows her stuff! (Rosa Burrell)

ENDNOTES

Introduction

1. J. Strong, *Strong's Exhaustive Concordance of the Bible* (Grand Rapids: Baker Book House, 1992), s.v. "damah."

Chapter 2
Dance: What Is It?

1. *Webster's New World Dictionary, Third College Edition*, s.v. "dance."

2. *Encyclopedia Britannica Online*, s.v. "dance." Can be viewed at http://www.britannica/EBchecked/topic/150714/dance (accessed October 15, 2010).

3. *Vine's Expository Dictionary of Biblical Words,* s.v. "to rejoice." (Nashville: Thomas Nelson Publishers, 1985), 196-197.

Chapter 3
The Creator of the Dance and Its Purpose

1. Myles Munroe, *In Pursuit of Purpose* (Shippensburg, PA: Destiny Image Publishers, 1992), 1.

2. *Vine's Expository Dictionary of Biblical Words*, s.v. "create."

3. J. Strong, *Strong's Exhaustive Concordance of the Bible*, s.v. "tohuw."

4. Ibid., s.v. "bohuw."

5. Ibid., s.v. "teh-home."

Chapter 5
Dance as Praise and Worship

1. Definitions adapted from *Strong's Exhaustive Concordance of the Bible*, s.vv "yadah," "towdah," "halal," "zamar," "tehillah," "barak," "shabach."

Chapter 9
The Power of Unity

1. J. Strong, *Strong's Exhaustive Concordance*, s.v. "spoudazo."

Chapter 10
Instruments of Praise, Worship and Warfare

1. *Webster's New World Dictionary*, Third College Edition, s.v. "banner."

2. J. Strong, *Strong's Exhaustive Concordance*, s.v. "dagal."

3. Ibid., s.v. "mishbar."

About the Author

Dr. Caretha Franks Crawford is the founding pastor and apostle of The Gateway to Wholeness Church Ministries in Largo, Md, a multifacted, non-denominational ministry dedicated to "Rebuilding Broken Lives Through the Power of Jesus Christ." She has organized and established Caretha Crawford Ministries International; The Gateway School of Pastoral Nurture International; The Pool of Bethseda, a healing school; Renewed Hope Community Development Corporation; and In Pursuit of His Presence Worship Institute, a Spirit-led training center that provides biblically-based education and mentorship to a generation of individuals who desire to consistently pursue the presence of God through the arts.

Dr. Crawford, a vivacious speaker, teacher, dance minister, author, publisher and conference convener, accepted Christ as her Lord and Savior while in her teens. She was licensed to preach the gospel in September 1994 and was ordained to the service of the Lord in September 1998 by Maple Springs Baptist Church of Capitol Heights, Md., where Rev. Chester A. McDonald, Sr. was the Pastor. She was the first woman to be licensed by the then 35-year-old church and the only woman, to date, to be ordained by this church.

Dr. Crawford was consecrated and elevated to the office of apostle in 2005. She preaches, teaches, and ministers the Word of God nationally and internationally. Her travels have taken her to London, England; Braunwald and Zurich, Switzerland; Nigeria and Sierra Leone, West Africa; Johannesburg, South Africa; Israel, Jordan, Egypt; Paris, France; Florence and Rome, Italy.

Dr. Crawford received a Bachleor of Science degree in Early Childhood Education from Winston-Salem State University, Winston-Salem, N.C. She holds earned Master of Biblical Studies, Master of Divinity and Doctor of Ministry degrees. Her careers include working as a public school kindergarten teacher and designing children clothing with designs sold in high-end stores such as Bloomingdale's, and sold and exhibited as far as Puerto Rico and Paris, France. She also served as an Assoicate Professor of Bible and Theology at Maple Springs Baptist Bible College and Seminary for six years.

As a successful entrepreneur, Dr. Crawford is the founder/CEO, designer and publisher of Kingdom Greetings 4U®, a line of handmade Christian greeting cards with "Inspiring Messages for the Royal Priesthood®." As an extension of this business venture, she established a non-profit organization, *Women Lifting Women Business Network*, to inspire, encourage, educate and motivate women to use their gifts and talents to expand the kingdom of God.

Dr. Crawford is married to Pastor Clarence Crawford. They are proud parents of one young adult daughter, Caletha Crawford.

For information about Dr. Caretha Crawford and her ministries, please contact at:

Caretha Crawford Ministries International
P. O. Box 6659
Largo, MD 20792

301.459.3680
email: drccrawford@earthlink.net or info@
carethacrawford.com
visit: www.carethacrawford.com

Author's Note

About Kathy Hazzard

From Michael Jackson to Elton John, from Diana Ross to Madonna, and from Yolanda Adams to Andrae Crouch…Kathy has sung with the best of them, and her talent continues to explode with conviction and power.

Kathy's professional career began with a contemporary gospel group called "Sweet Spirit." The group was comprised of four young ladies from New York and was discovered by gospel legend Andrae Crouch. They recorded a self-titled album that achieved national and international success. Kathy later became a member of Andrae's group, "The Disciples" and continues to tour throughout the world with them.

While enjoying a very successful singing career, Kathy discovered the emergence of several other gifts and talents. Her love for the theater, television, film, fashion and public speaking would soon be in competition with her singing. She has appeared on numerous television shows and movies such as "The Color Purple," "Amen," "L.A. Law," "Free Willy," "Doogie Howser," "NYPD Blue," "Women of Brewster Place," "Martin," "VIBE," and "Sister, Sister." She has also made appearances on "The Young and the Restless,"

"Hercules," "Cats Don't Dance," "The Lion King," "Lion King II," "Mighty Joe Young" and "The Hughleys."

Kathy is also the singing voice behind the popular TV show "Silk Stalkings." She can be heard on the K-Mart, Big Red, Mobil Oil, Campbell's Soup, Kraft and Coca-Cola commercials, as well. Most recently, along with the Andrae Crouch singers, she did all the vocals (including the opening song) for Michael Jackson's memorial service.

In January 2000, CNN'S "Showbiz Today" chose her as one of the most distinctive voices of the 90's in background music during its entertainment review on "Unsung Heroes."

Her love for God is seen in the way she carries the grace and mercy of the Lord in every arena God brings her to; and she continues to touch lives where many have not gone and cannot go. Always moving forward, Kathy is currently in the process of pitching a sitcom/drama that she created to the networks.

Breinigsville, PA USA
07 January 2011
252877BV00002B/2/P